gage Cornerstones

CANADIAN LANGUAGE ARTS

Anthology 5b

gage EDUCATIONAL PUBLISHING COMPANY
A DIVISION OF CANADA PUBLISHING CORPORATION
Vancouver · Calgary · Toronto · London · Halifax

Canadian Cataloguing in Publication Data

Main entry under title:

Gage cornerstones: Canadian language arts. Anthology, 5b

Includes index.
ISBN 0-7715-1209-0

1. Readers (Elementary).   I. McClymont, Christine.
II. Title: Cornerstones: Canadian language arts.
III. Title: Anthology, 5b

PE1121.G26 1998   428.6   C98-930974-6

Researchers: Todd Mercer, Monika Croydon, Monica Kulling

Cover Illustration: Simon Ng

Acknowledgments

Every reasonable effort has been made to trace ownership of copyrighted material. Information that would enable the publisher to correct any reference or credit in future editions would be appreciated.

7 "Picking Teams" from *Please Mrs. Butler* by Allan Ahlberg. © 1983 by Penguin Books, UK. / 8-13 "The Magic Baseball Card" by Jim Prime. © 1989 by Jim Prime. By permission of the author. / 16 "The Grandstander" by Anne Haeusler from *Slam Dunk: Basketball Poems* compiled by Lillian Morrison. © 1994 by Anne Haeusler. / 18-21 "Duos on Ice" by Patty Cranston and Allison Gertridge, excerpts from *Superstars on Ice* by Patty Cranston. Text © 1996 by Patty Cranston. By permission of Kids Can Press Ltd., Toronto. / 24-25 "Cool Inuit Games" from *Owl Magazine* (April 1994), Vol 19, No. 4. / 28 "Culture" from *Meet Danitra Brown* by Nikki Grimes. Illustrated by Floyd Cooper. Text © 1994 by Nikki Grimes. Illustrations © 1994 by Floyd Cooper. By permission of Lothrop, Lee & Shepard Books, a division of William Morrow & Company. 30-33 "Barn Raising" from *A People Apart* by Kathleen Kenna, photographs by Andrew Stawicki, A Nick Harris Book, Somerville House Books Limited, Toronto, 1995. / 36-43 "Three Monks, No Water" by Ting-xing Ye. Text © 1997 by Ting-xing Ye. Illustrations © 1997 by Harvey Chan. By permission of Annick Press Ltd. / 49 "Telephone Talk" from *The Kite That Braved Old Orchard Beach* by X.J. Kennedy. © 1991 by X.J. Kennedy. By permission of Margaret K. McElderry Books, an imprint of Simon & Schuster Children's Publishing Division. / 52-53 "Before Telephones" from *The Phone Book* by Elizabeth MacLeod, illustrated by Bill Slavin. Text © 1995 by Elizabeth MacLeod. Illustrations © 1995 by Bill Slavin. By permission of Kids Can Press Ltd., Toronto. / 56-63 "Sweet Clara and the Freedom Quilt" by Deborah Hopkinson. Text © 1993 by Deborah Hopkinson. Illustrations © 1993 by James Ransome. / 66-69 "Cowboyspeak" from *Cowboy: A Kid's Album* by Linda Granfield. © 1993 by Linda Granfield. By permission of Douglas & McIntyre Ltd. / 72 "Jimmy Jet and His TV Set" from *Where the Sidewalk Ends* by Shel Silverstein. © 1974 by Evil Eye Music, Inc. / 74-77 "We'll Be Right Back After These Messages" from *The TV Book* by Shelagh Wallace. Text © 1996 by Shelagh Wallace. Illustrations © 1996 by Lorraine Tuson and Brian Bean. By permission of Annick Press Ltd. / 80-83 "Birthday Box" by Jane Yolen from *Birthday Surprises: Ten Great Stories to Unwrap*, published by Morrow Junior Books. © 1995 by Jane Yolen. By permission of Curtis Brown Ltd. / 87 "It's Not Fair" by Jonathan Schwartz. By permission of Jonathan Schwartz. / 90-99 "The Grade Five Lie" from *Little by Little* by Jean Little. © 1987 by Jean Little. By permission of Penguin Books Canada Ltd. / 102 "The Right Thing" from Calvin and Hobbes by Bill Watterson. © 1993 by Bill Watterson. Distributed by Universal Press Syndicate. Reprinted by permission. All rights reserved. / 104-111 "How Smudge Came" by Nan Gregory. Illustrations by Ron

Lightburn. Text © 1995 by Nan Gregory. Illustrations © 1995 by Ron Lightburn. By permission of Red Deer College Press. / 114 "Prejudice is Something We Can Do Without" from *Inu and Indians We're Called* by Rita Joe. © 1991 by Rita Joe, published by Ragweed Press, Charlottetown, PEI. By permission of the publisher. / 116-121 "Children Who Work" from *Listen to Us: The World's Working Children* by Jane Springer. © 1997 by Jane Springer. A Groundwood Book/Douglas & McIntyre. / 124-129 "The Saltbox Sweater" by Janet McNaughton. © 1998 by Janet McNaughton. By permission of the author. / 133-134 "Dr. Quicksolve's Whodunit Puzzles" from *Quicksolve Whodunit Puzzles* by Jim Sukach. © 1995 by Jim Sukach. By permission of Sterling Publishing Co., Inc., c/o Canadian Manda Group, One Atlantic Ave., Ste. 105, Toronto, Ont., M6K 3E7. / 136-139 Cover illustrations © Pat Cupples. Excerpts and photos © Linda Bailey. / 142-151 "The Red-Headed League" from *Mysteries of Sherlock Holmes* by Sir Arthur Conan Doyle, adapted by Judith Conaway. Text © 1982 by Random House, Inc. Illustrations © 1982 by Lyle Miller. By permission of Random House, Inc. / 154-157 Excerpts from *The Mysteries of Harris Burdick* by Chris Van Allsburg. © 1984 by Chris Van Allsburg. By permission of Houghton Mifflin Co. All rights reserved.

Photo Credits

6-7 David Young Wolff/Tony Stone; 7 Juan Silva/Image Bank; **15, 65, 88, 130, 153** Dave Starrett; **18 top, 19 inset, 20 top, 20 bottom, 21, 23 top left** Cam Silverson; **18 bottom, 19 top, 23 top right, 23 bottom left, 23 bottom right** Barb McCutcheon; **24-25** Tony Thomas; **46** Peter McEwan; **48-49** Michael Alberstadt; **68-69** Mike Drew, Calgary; **70 left** Glenbow Archives, Calgary, Canada (NC-19-6); **70 right, 71** John McQuarrie; **73** Chip Henderson/Tony Stone Images; **74** Macpherson/Tony Stone Images; **75** Shoot Pty-TCL/Masterfile; **76** Graham French/Masterfile; **77** William Sallaz/Image Bank; **116, 117, 118** Reebok International Ltd.; **120, 121** Toronto Star Syndicate; **152 top, bottom** Everett Collection.

Illustrations

26, 45 Dan Hobbs; **29, 84, 101** Steve Attoe; **35, 50-51, 74-77, 79** Bill Suddick; **54-55** Norman Eyolfson; **86-87** Jun Park; **89** Pronk&Associates; **113** Ron Lightburn; **132** John Etheridge; **141** Pat Cupples; **142** Tom Newsom.

ISBN 0-7715-**1209**-0
2 3 4 5 6 BP 04 03 02 01 00 99
Printed and bound in Canada.

Cornerstones Development Team

HERE ARE THE PEOPLE WHO WORKED HARD TO MAKE THIS BOOK EXCITING FOR YOU!

WRITING TEAM

Christine McClymont
Patrick Lashmar
Dennis Strauss
Patricia FitzGerald-Chesterman
Cam Colville
Robert Cutting
Stephen Hurley
Luigi Iannacci
Oksana Kuryliw
Caroline Lutyk

GAGE EDITORIAL

Joe Banel
Rivka Cranley
Elizabeth Long
David MacDonald
Evelyn Maksimovich
Diane Robitaille
Darleen Rotozinski
Jennifer Stokes
Carol Waldock

GAGE PRODUCTION

Anna Kress
Bev Crann

DESIGN, ART DIRECTION & ELECTRONIC ASSEMBLY

Pronk&Associates

ADVISORY TEAM

Connie Fehr Burnaby SD, BC
Elizabeth Sparks Delta SD, BC
John Harrison Burnaby SD, BC
Joan Alexander St. Albert PSSD, AB
Carol Germyn Calgary B of E, AB
Cathy Sitko Edmonton Catholic SD, AB
Laura Haight Saskatoon SD, SK
Linda Nosbush Prince Albert SD, SK
Linda Tysowski Saskatoon PSD, SK
Maureen Rodniski Winnipeg SD, MB
Cathy Saytar Dufferin-Peel CDSB, ON
Jan Adams Thames Valley DSB, ON
Linda Ross Thames Valley DSB, ON
John Cassano York Region DSB, ON
Carollynn Desjardins Nipissing-Parry Sound
    CDSB, ON
David Hodgkinson Waterloo Region DSB, ON
Michelle Longlade Halton CDSB, ON
Sharon Morris Toronto CDSB, ON
Heather Sheehan Toronto CDSB, ON
Ruth Scott Brock University, ON
Elizabeth Thorn Nipissing University, ON
Jane Abernethy Chipman & Fredericton SD, NB
Darlene Whitehouse-Sheehan Chipman &
    Fredericton SD, NB
Carol Chandler Halifax Regional SB, NS
Martin MacDonald Strait Regional Board, NS
Ray Doiron University of PEI, PE
Robert Dawe Avalon East SD, NF
Margaret Ryall Avalon East SD, NF

Contents

Teamwork

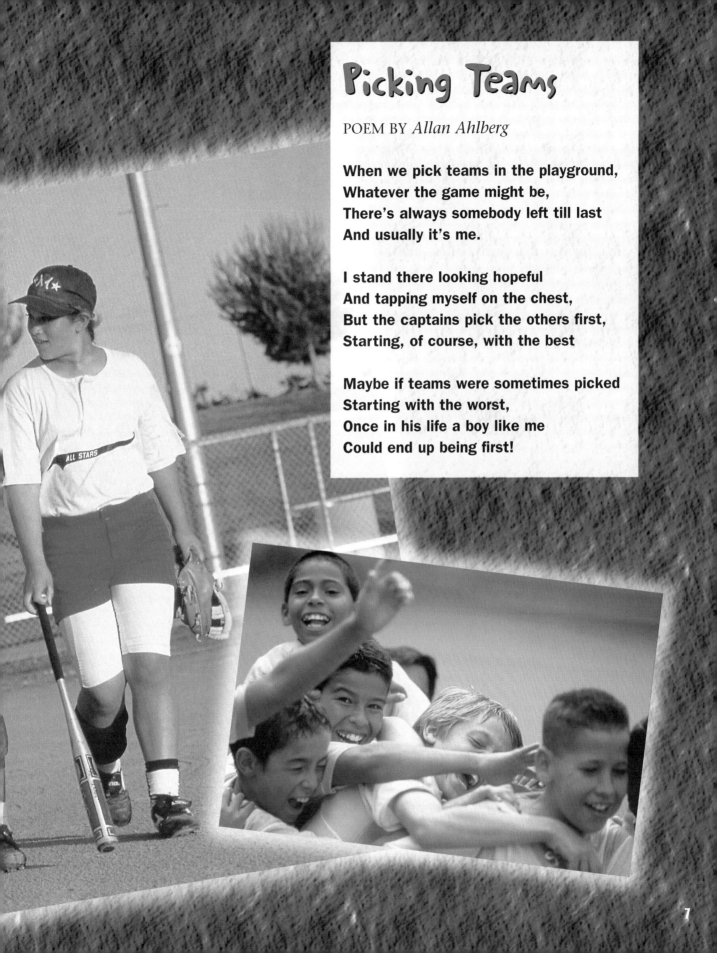

Picking Teams

POEM BY *Allan Ahlberg*

When we pick teams in the playground,
Whatever the game might be,
There's always somebody left till last
And usually it's me.

I stand there looking hopeful
And tapping myself on the chest,
But the captains pick the others first,
Starting, of course, with the best

Maybe if teams were sometimes picked
Starting with the worst,
Once in his life a boy like me
Could end up being first!

Teamwork

Ted Williams was a great player for the Boston Red Sox. He inspired generations of baseball fans, including the author, Jim Prime. Read on to discover why he was a hero to Jeffrey, the boy in this story.

The Magic Baseball Card

Story by **JIM PRIME**   *Pictures by* **BRIAN DEINES**

Playing baseball on a small Nova Scotia island in the Bay of Fundy presents some special problems. For one thing, there's the fog. It creeps slowly across the field, swallowing first the outfielders, then the second baseman, and finally the pitcher.

Jeffrey Curtis hated playing ball in the fog. He heard the crack of the bat and knew the ball was coming toward centre field. But he couldn't see it. Then—at the last split second—he flicked his glove toward a round white blur and grabbed it for the final out in the top of the ninth.

"We need radar out here," Jeffrey yelled to his friend Marc, as they jogged in for their turn at bat.

"Count your blessings," called Marc. "At least the outfield is fairly level. This infield makes the surface of the moon look like a putting green."

Jeffrey was first up at bat. Someone yelled, "Smoke one for the Schooners, Jeffrey." He smiled and patted his hip pocket. His good-luck piece was still there. It was only a bubblegum card—a laminated rectangle of cardboard. It had a picture of a baseball player on one side and the player's life history on the other. But this was no ordinary card. This was a 1956 Ted Williams, given to him by his grandfather just a few weeks before his granddad died.

Jeffrey and his grandfather had spent many long hours together talking about baseball—today's baseball and the baseball of forty years ago. They disagreed about domed stadiums, artificial turf, and the DH* rule. But they both agreed that Ted Williams had been the greatest hitter of all time.

Jeffrey felt powerful with the bat in his hands and the card in his pocket. He stepped into the batter's box and squinted through the fog at the Westport Whitecaps' pitcher.

The first pitch was waist-high and just a little inside. He jumped on it, driving it deep into right field. As he rounded first base, he could see the ball drop just beyond the outfielder's reach. Between second and third he made up his mind to try to beat the throw to the plate. The second baseman took the relay and fired homeward, but Jeffrey slid in under the catcher's tag for the winning run. Final score: Freeport Schooners 3–Westport Whitecaps 2. The card had come through again.

---

* designated hitter

The Magic Baseball Card   **9**

*W*hen Jeffrey got home after the game that afternoon, he knew that something was up. His father and his sister Catherine were sitting at the kitchen table looking over maps and brochures. His father looked up and smiled.

"What was the score?" he asked.

"Three-two for the good guys," said Jeffrey. "What's going on here?"

Just then he saw a brochure with the words *Things to Do in Boston* on the front. His heart beat faster.

"We're planning our vacation," said his dad, still grinning.

Without thinking, Jeffrey felt for the Ted Williams card and tapped it three times for luck. They were going to see some ball games. He just knew it.

Catherine looked up from a list she was making. "I'm going to Boston to visit Mom, and you and Dad are going fishing," she said.

Jeffrey looked from his sister to his father. This had to be a joke. But his dad was nodding his head.

"That's right. We're going salmon fishing on the Miramichi River in New Brunswick. What do you think of that?"

Since the news was announced like a present, Jeffrey tried to act pleased. But he wasn't. It was as if Ted Williams had struck out with the bases loaded.

Catherine is going to be in Boston watching Red Sox games with Mom, while I'm up the creek with Dad, he thought. *And Catherine likes the Expos—she's not even a Red Sox fan!*

A couple of weeks later, Jeffrey looked out of the window of the log cabin his father had rented on the Miramichi. The morning sun was sending shafts of light through the pine trees. It was 6:05 a.m., and his father was standing over a pan of sizzling bacon and eggs. They sat at the table and ate in silence. Finally his father spoke.

"I know you'd rather have gone to Boston, see the Red Sox play and all that. I just thought... Well, I know I've been on the road a lot the last few years. I thought it would be nice for the two of us to spend some time together."

Jeffrey was surprised. He hadn't really thought about how often his dad was away from home. Maybe because he'd had

Granddad. But more than that, he had thought he had been able to hide his feelings about not going to Boston.

"It's OK, Dad," he said, forcing a smile. "Red Sox fans are used to disappointments."

"I know you miss your grandfather. You two were always together. I miss him, too. He was my dad, remember. And you'll be happy to know that he taught me a little about baseball. Did you know that Ted Williams hit a home run in his last time at bat?"

Of course Jeffrey knew. But he had no idea that his dad knew stuff like that.

His father continued, "Did you know he was the last ballplayer to hit .400 in a season?"

Jeffrey smiled patiently. "Dad, I don't want to hurt your feelings, but I think I know everything there is to know about Ted Williams."

It was his father's turn to smile patiently. "Maybe so," he said, "but we'll see. Before our week is over you just might learn something new."

By 7:15 they were at the river, casting for Atlantic salmon. Jeffrey was surprised to see the long smooth casts his father made. As they fished, they talked baseball. Every so often there would be another Ted Williams question.

"Did you know that he hit a home run every sixteen times at bat on average?"

"Yes, Dad, I knew that," said Jeffrey. But even though he knew all the answers, it was great to have someone to talk baseball with again.

"Do you still have that card that your grandfather gave you?" asked his father.

Jeffrey was a little embarrassed. He didn't think anyone knew about the card.

"Yes, I've got it with me." He reached into his pocket, but when he pulled the card out, it slipped through his wet fingers and dropped into the fast-moving river.

He made a grab for it, but he couldn't move fast enough in his clumsy hip waders.

"Get it, Dad!" he yelled, but it was too late. The plastic-coated card was bobbing wildly in the current.

"We've got to get it back!" he cried desperately.

"The river narrows below here," his father said as they clambered toward the shore. "Maybe it'll snag on the rocks." He didn't sound very hopeful.

As they made their way around the river's bed, they saw a tall man bending to scoop something from the water. He examined it closely and started to laugh.

Just then the man saw Jeffrey and his father on the shore.

"Is this yours?" the man asked, wading toward the shore. There was a smile on his tanned face. Somehow the face looked familiar, Jeffrey thought, like a long-ago friend who had got older.

"Yes, sir," he panted. His voice was ragged with relief. "It slipped out of my hand. It's my good luck card. My grandfather gave it to me." Jeffrey realized he was babbling and stopped abruptly.

"Is this guy your dad?" asked the tall man.

"Yes, sir." He waited for his father to introduce himself, but instead, the two men shook hands like old friends.

"Then you must be Jeffrey—the ballplayer."

Jeffrey looked puzzled.

"Maybe I'd better explain, son," said his dad. "This is... Ted Williams."

Jeffrey looked as if he had seen a ghost. The man standing on the shore holding his Ted Williams baseball card *was* Ted Williams. "No wonder you looked familiar," he stammered, "but..."

"I told you that you might learn something new this week," said Jeffrey's dad. "I bet you didn't know that Ted Williams has had a camp on this river since 1955."

"I sure didn't," beamed Jeffrey.

The rest of the day he talked baseball and fishing with his dad and Ted Williams. For him, it was like a dream come true.

That night, as they made their way back to their cabin, Jeffrey pulled the baseball card from his pocket. In one short day he had met his hero, Ted Williams, and discovered a new friend to talk baseball with—his dad.

The magic was still alive. ⬡

FOLLOW UP

Why was Ted Williams a hero to Jeffrey? Do you think Jeffrey discovered a new hero by the end of the story?

Teamwork at Home

Take this story home for the grown-ups to enjoy. Some might even have heard of Ted Williams. Talk about the ideas of teamwork that come up in the story, and how they could apply in your family.

IMAGINE!

What do you and your classmates collect: sports cards, stickers, stamps, hats? Organize an exhibition with space to display and talk about your collections.

Understanding the Story

Hit One for the Schooners!

- What did Jeffrey mean when he told Marc they needed radar on the baseball field?

- Explain why Jeffrey's baseball card was so important to him.

- Why was Jeffrey unhappy about the family's holiday plans? Why did he try to hide his feelings?

- How did Jeffrey's father explain why he brought Jeffrey on the fishing trip?

- In what ways did the baseball card produce "magic" for Jeffrey?

Design a Uniform

Team members often wear a uniform to show they belong. Your task is to design a uniform for the Schooners or the Whitecaps. It takes teamwork to come up with a good design. Form small groups. Ask team members what their special talents are: getting ideas, drawing logos, writing letters, choosing colours, and so on. Then work together (co-operate) to design a uniform for your players.

Sports Announcers

You and a partner are the broadcast team announcing the game between the Schooners and the Whitecaps. Together, write the script you will follow, using names and details from the story to give a clear picture of what happened. You can also add details of your own. Practise reading your script aloud in "sportscaster" voices. When you're ready, "announce" the game to a group of friends!

Sports Go to the Movies

CLASS DISCUSSION

Movies about baseball, basketball, football, and hockey are popular. What movies have you seen? Which one is your favourite? Make a class list of the top ten sports movies.

The Grandstander

Poem by *Anne Haeusler*
Pictures by *Heather Holbrook*

The score was tied
with a minute to go.
Ball caught at midcourt—
she poised for the throw,
a two-handed shot,
a perfect long loop.
Unbelievable!
Right into the hoop.
She should have passed
but all the same
her team forgave her
for winning the game.

Compare Two Poems

Compare *The Grandstander* with *Picking Teams* on page 7. In each poem, someone has difficulty being part of a team. But the reasons are very different. With a partner, talk about these differences.

- What problem does the speaker in *Picking Teams* have with the way teams work?
- What is a "grandstander"? How did the grandstander in the poem break the rules of her team sport, basketball?
- Do you agree that the goal of team sports is winning? How do these poems illustrate this idea?

Something To Think About

"The bonds on this team are strong. These women are unbelievably committed to one another."

– Coach of Canada's Women's Hockey team.

To play a team sport, you need teamwork—players working together and playing by the rules. Think of your favourite team sport. When is close teamwork most necessary? When is it OK for a player to break out on his or her own, as the "Grandstander" did?

Act It Out – Mime!

Mime is a form of acting that uses movement and gestures, but no words. In a group of two or three "players," reread *The Grandstander* and imagine how you could mime the poem. Practise physical actions and facial expressions that will help you to tell the story. Begin with catching the ball, then mime all the actions through to celebrating the win. When you are ready, perform your mime for the class.

Who are the most exciting figure skaters you've ever seen? Preview the article to find out which skaters you will read about, which country they skate for, and what medals they have won.

Duos on Ice

Profiles by
PATTY CRANSTON
AND
ALLISON GERTRIDGE

In pairs skating, two skaters not only perform exciting lifts and moves—such as a death spiral, shown here—as a team, but they must also be able to jump, spin, and do difficult footwork in unison. Isabelle Brasseur and Lloyd Eisler of Canada are especially known for skating in perfect time with each other.

*Isabelle Brasseur
& Lloyd Eisler*

CANADA
Olympic Bronze, 1992, 1994
World Champions, 1993

*Jayne Torvill
& Christopher Dean*

GREAT BRITAIN
Olympic Champions, 1984
Olympic Bronze, 1994
World Champions, 1981-1984

Ice dancers, such as Jayne Torvill and Christopher Dean of Great Britain, base their routines on ballroom dances. They have to follow strict rules about the type of jumps and lifts allowed in their routines. Another rule says that dancers aren't allowed to separate more than five times during their program. Smooth, innovative, and clever, Torvill and Dean tell a story with their music.

Shae-Lynn Bourne & Victor Kraatz

CANADA

Canadian Champions, 1993-1997
3rd at World Championships, 1996-1998

Just days before Skate Canada in 1995, Victor accidentally slashed Shae-Lynn's leg. At the competition, she skated with seventeen stitches —all the way to gold.

You want edges? They've got 'em. Style? They have that, too. And with five national championship titles to their credit, Shae-Lynn Bourne and Victor Kraatz have trophies enough to make any competitor nervous.

These ice dancers continue to perfect their hydroblading, a technique in which the pair skate almost parallel to the ice, using each other for support. Their unique style enables them to use the edges of their blades in a way that few other skaters can.

In the past, some judges have criticized Victor and Shae-Lynn for their unconventional moves, like skating low to the ice. But fans around the world think these exciting Canadians have injected new life into the dance arena.

"They show that big winning athletes can be excellent people too. It's important to me who deserves to be champion. They do."

Coach Natalia Dubova

Ekaterina Gordeeva & Sergei Grinkov

RUSSIA

Olympic Champions, 1988, 1994
World Champions, 1986, 1987, 1989, 1990

The skating world lost one of its best performers with the sudden and unexpected death of Sergei Grinkov in November 1995. Ekaterina Gordeeva and Sergei Grinkov were two of the most talented pairs skaters ever, and they seemed to skate better every time they performed.

This pair had it all: speed, power, flow, and grace. When they skated, "G & G" made their spectacular throws and majestic lifts look effortless. During a jump or throw triple—a move in which the man throws his partner into the air, she rotates three times and then lands on one foot—they could maintain the same speed on the exit from the move as they had on the entry. Keeping that speed requires great skill because in order to throw his partner, the man must dig hard into the ice without going too far forward on his toe picks or they will slow him down.

In 1986, G & G won their first World Championships when "Katya" was only fourteen, and just two years later they struck gold at the Olympics. Gordeeva and Grinkov turned professional in 1990, but soon missed the challenge of amateur competition. Their comeback was golden when they won the 1994 Olympics. Sadly, G & G will never skate together again, but the memories of the magic they created on ice will make them legends forever.

"It's just a huge shock," said pairs skater Lloyd Eisler about Grinkov's death, "and the skating world and the fans have lost someone who cannot be replaced." ⬡

"Gordeeva and Grinkov were in a league by themselves. What set them apart was their refinement, caring, and tenderness for each other. They were everything pairs skating should be."

Sandra Bezic, 1995
Choreographer and commentator

Which of the figure skating duos in the article did you find the most interesting? Which would you most like to see skating?

Understanding the Article

Lifts and Throws

Each of the duos in the article has a special talent, a unique appeal to the audience. Write a sentence in your notebook about each duo to describe what makes them distinctive.

Skaters	Ice Dance or Pairs	Description
Brasseur & Eisler		
Torvill & Dean		
Bourne & Kraatz		
Gordeeva & Grinkov		

Trusting Your Partner

SMALL GROUP DISCUSSION

Skating duos are a good example of one kind of teamwork: the need to trust your partner completely. Discuss why this is true, based on the article and skaters you have seen on television.

Now make a list of other kinds of activities that require absolute trust in a partner. Think about sports, circuses, recreational activities, and performing arts. Why do you think people who do these activities work so hard and take such risks?

Viewing the Photographs

You are an action-photo judge. Choose the photographs you find most exciting. Assign them the gold, the silver, and the bronze medal. Cut large round medals out of cardboard. On each one, write notes about why you chose the photo as a winner. Collect all the "medals" and choose the overall class winners!

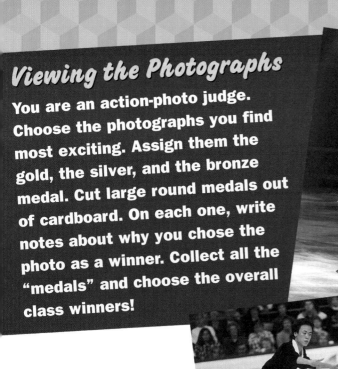

Developing Vocabulary

Some verbs can be turned into nouns by adding the suffix **-tion, -ation,** or **-ition**. Before adding the suffix, you may need to change the spelling of the base word. In your notebooks, turn the following verbs into nouns and add the meanings of the nouns. Use a dictionary to help you. The first one has been done for you.

VERB	NOUN	MEANING
rotate	rotation	turning in a circle
compete		
continue		
separate		
create		

IMAGINE!

Calling all skaters! With a partner, create a one-minute pairs or dance program on ice. Choose music, appropriate costumes, and work out the choreography.

What games do you play in which winning is not important?

Cool Inuit Games

W hat does it take to survive in the North? Plenty of strength and endurance—just what you'll find in these ancient games. Give them a try and see if you're fit for the traditional Inuit way of life!

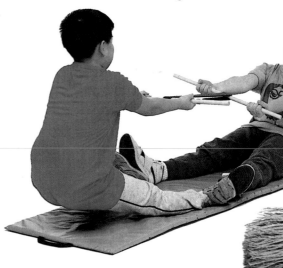

Article from
OWL MAGAZINE

Ac Sa Raq
[ahk saah rahq]
(Thong Game)

You'll need a strong leather belt and two short poles. Sit with your legs straight and your feet against your opponent's. Now try to pull your opponent up and off the ground using the belt and poles. *Ac Sa Raq* develops strength in your arms.

Tirusuraqtut Aqupiutanin
[tee roo soo rahg tooq ah qoo pew tah neen]
(Kneel Reach)

Kneel on the floor and ask a friend to sit on your feet. With one hand behind your back, place a block on the floor in front of you, as far away as you can reach. Return to an upright position. Be sure not to touch the floor with your hands at any time. *Tirusuraqtut Aqupiutanin* develops strength and endurance in your torso and lower body.

Tiliraginik Qiriqtagtut
[tee lee rah gee neek qeeg geerq tanq toot]
(Jump Through Stick)

Hold a long stick in front of you with your hands the width of your shoulders apart. Jump over the stick without letting it go and land on both feet, well-balanced. Repeat the jump backwards. *Tiliraginik Qiriqtagtut* develops your flexibility.

Tu Nu Miu
[too noo mew]
(Back Push)

Mark a line on the floor or a mat. Sit there back-to-back with your opponent so that the line runs between you. The object of the game is to be the first to cross over the line. You can only use your hands and feet for balance and leverage. *Tu Nu Miu* develops strength and endurance in your torso, legs, and lower body.

WARNING:
These games are like any other kinds of exercise—don't overdo them. If you've got neck or back problems, get permission to do them from your parent or doctor. Build your strength gradually. And don't forget to warm up first!

Which of these Inuit games looks like the most fun to try?

Understanding the Article

Strength and Endurance

- Which of these Inuit games requires a partner, and which can be done by an individual?

- Which of the games could have a winner?

- Which of the games is non-competitive?

- Besides fun, what benefit would you gain from playing each of these games?

- Make a list of the equipment you would need to play these games.

Hold the Cool Games Olympics

Plan to use the gym for this event. With the help of your teacher, organize yourselves into teams of four. To prepare for the games, your team will need to

- select a coach
- learn to play the Inuit games and your invented games
- practise the games
- decide which team member will enter each event

When you are ready, make a poster for the Cool Games Olympics. Design medals for (a) games that have a winner and (b) games that are demonstrations of skill. Perhaps you could invite friends and family to come and watch. Enjoy!

Language Study

In the article, each set of instructions has the following elements:

- how to get ready
- how to use the equipment
- how to play the game
- the benefit you receive from playing the game

Instructions also use command verbs:
sit, lie down, kneel.

Reread two sets of instructions and locate these elements.

IMAGINE!

Think of traditional Inuit methods of transportation and getting food. How would these games help to prepare the people for such tasks?

Instructions for a Game

STEP 1: Choose a partner. Your task is to invent a game which develops strength and endurance, using simple equipment.

STEP 2: Write out instructions for playing your game. Follow the examples in the article.

STEP 3: Give your instructions to another pair of students. See if they can follow them! Make your instructions clearer, if necessary.

STEP 4: Add your game to a class Cool Games Book. Illustrate your instructions with drawings or photographs of students playing the game.

Something To Think About

Recent studies show that Canadian elementary school students are not very fit. Many are lacking in strength and endurance, and their health may suffer as they grow older. As a class, make a plan to increase your fitness levels.

Culture

POEM BY **Nikki Grimes**

PICTURE BY **Floyd Cooper**

Mom says I need culture, whatever that means;
then she irons some dumb dress, makes me take off my jeans,
drags me to the theatre for some stupid show.
(It turns out to be fun, but I don't let her know.)
Next day I tell Danitra what the play was about,
then we go to her bedroom and act it all out.
We play all of the parts, and pretend that we're stars
like the ones that step out of those long shiny cars.
Then Danitra starts dancing while I sing the main song,
and she promises that next time she'll come along.
We decide we like culture, whatever that means,
but we both think that culture goes better with jeans!

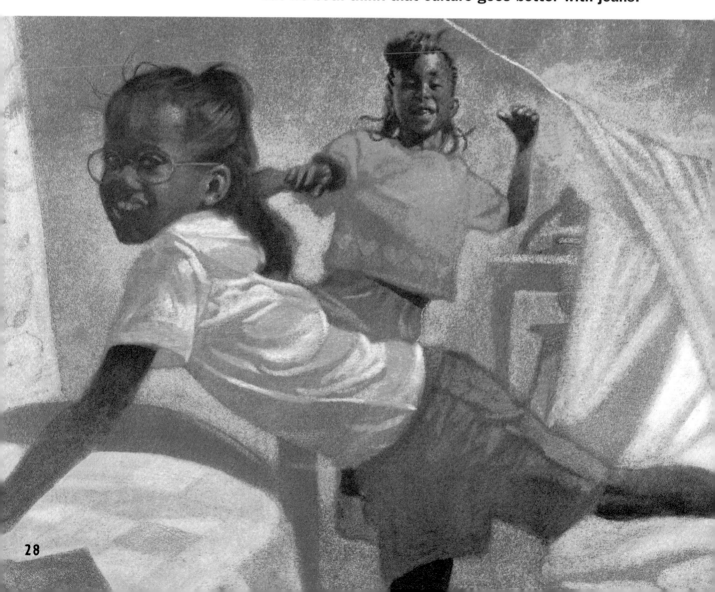

Personal Response

• Why was the speaker in the poem reluctant to go to the theatre with her mother? Would you have felt the same way?

• Why didn't she want to tell her mom that the show was fun?

• How did teaming up with Danitra help to change her mind about "culture"? Do you have a friend who makes everything more fun?

YOUR TURN TO WRITE

An Anecdote

Have you ever been involved in the performing arts—a class play, a school band, a choir, a dance, a music recital? How was teamwork important to the success of your performance? Write a short story about your personal experience of "Teamwork in the Performing Arts."

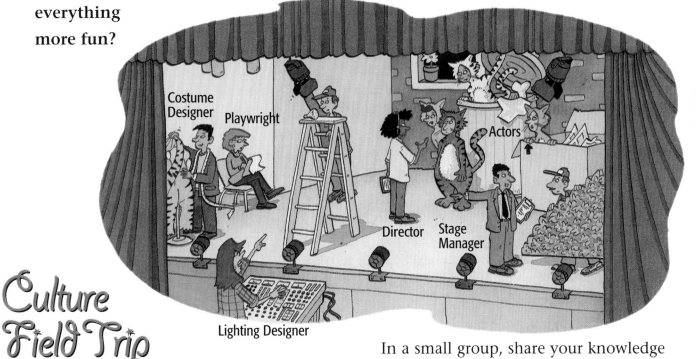

Costume Designer   Playwright   Actors   Director   Stage Manager   Lighting Designer

Culture Field Trip

In the theatre, it takes many people working together to produce a play. Here are some of the jobs in theatre:

☆ the playwright
☆ the director
☆ the lighting designer
☆ the costume designer
☆ the stage manager
☆ the actors

In a small group, share your knowledge of the important jobs each of these people do. In what ways do they need to work together to put on a play? Then, if possible, attend a live performance of a play. Or, invite someone who has worked in the theatre to talk to the class about putting on plays.

Think about what it takes to build a barn. What materials would be needed? What jobs would people do? What equipment would they use? How long would it take?

congregation: a group of people gathered together for religious worship.

Barn Raising

ARTICLE BY *Kathleen Kenna*

PHOTOGRAPHS BY *Andrew Stawicki*

Old Order Mennonites are Christians who decided to live in separate communities 500 years ago. Most families do without modern conveniences such as cars and electricity. Mennonites harvest crops with horse-drawn equipment and cook on woodburning stoves. The children study in Old Order schools, and wear clothes very like those the pioneers wore 100 years ago. Young people who choose to stay in the community look forward to a secure future with a close circle of friends and family.

Aside from their commitment to peace, one of the most important Old Order beliefs among the Mennonites is the importance of helping others. Mennonites raise money for the poor, dig wells in developing countries, and volunteer after natural disasters like hurricanes. But while Old Order Mennonites send money and sometimes workers to help the needy

Mennonite girls dressed in traditional clothes walk to school.

The heavy sides of this new barn were built flat on the ground before they were pulled upright with ropes.

outside their community, they generally follow the old saying "charity begins at home."

Nowhere is this sense of community more remarkable than at a barn raising. Since an Old Order family has no insurance, a barn fire could ruin them financially. Instead, a crew of men raise a barn from the ashes in little more than a day.

After one winter blaze, dozens of men and boys from ten different Mennonite congregations gathered at the farm. Construction was delayed by cold rain, and farmers delivered lumber and other supplies to the farm while they waited for the weather to clear. In kitchens across the countryside, Old Order women baked pies, bread, and other foods.

The call came early in the morning to Onias Metzger, who told some families by telephone. Families without phones were sent for by horse-and-buggy messenger. The men arrived, and the work continued from early morning until almost dark.

A man balances on the top of the new barn.

All day, the singsong of hammers and saws cracked the cold air, while men sweated over a mammoth wooden frame. A chief carpenter helped organize the work crews, directing the strongest builders to one corner, telling boys to haul nails to another. The barn skeleton took shape quickly from a tangle of men and tools and lumber. The carpenters, almost all farmers, fell into a natural rhythm, co-operating with few instructions and some friendly chatter. The younger men were so confident that they walked across high beams without safety harnesses.

As parts of the frame were ready to be raised, the men hoisted them into place without machinery, all shouting "Yo!" (Get ready) and "He!" (Push). Women spent hours preparing a huge meal for the lunch break. Tables were set up in the driving shed—a smaller barn used to store farm equipment— and the women served heaping plates of vegetables, meat, salads, and homemade bread. After the meal was finished, the men completed as much of the outer shell as possible before darkness. The indoor work and the roof were finished another day by some of the same volunteers.

The congregation later shared the cost of the barn materials. "You're not compelled to pay a certain amount if you can't," says Edwin Martin, whose buggy-making shop is not far from the new barn. Figuring he has probably seen more barn raisings than most Old Order Mennonites, he adds, "You give what you can afford and you pay so that you are satisfied in your own mind that you have helped as best you can."

FOLLOW UP

What surprised you about Mennonite barn raising? What new ideas did you learn from reading the article?

Understanding the Article

Raising the Roof

- Men, women, and children had different jobs to do on the day of the barn raising. What were they? Why do you think they had different roles?

- The photograph and caption on page 31 show how the men raised the barn frame. Explain in your own words how they did it.

- This article shows that Old Order Mennonites have a "strong sense of community." What does this phrase mean to you?

Career Tip

Do you think you would enjoy building things with wood? Carpentry is a useful skill that you can use all your life. Some people choose carpentry as a career, building everything from furniture to houses. If you're interested

- read books about wood and how to build with it

- take woodworking courses in high school

- try all kinds of projects using carpentry

Remember, carpenters know that you can "do-it-yourself"!

Brainstorming

As a class, talk about the way the Mennonite community used teamwork to solve a problem—how to raise a barn quickly. Then discuss other problems that could be solved by co-operation. Here are a few examples:

- litter beside a highway
- garbage tossed into a creek
- safety problems in a local park
- older people living in isolated places

How could you and your community get together to solve problems like these?

Teamwork Editing

Think about an event that involves co-operation among a group of people. It could be a family picnic, a club meeting, a birthday party, a sports day, a clean-up program, a choral festival, a performance of a play—you name it!

Choose an event in which you took part. Then write a report about it. Use these guidelines for your writing:

A: Write an opening sentence that catches the reader's attention.

B: Describe the event in a few sentences. Tell what jobs you and other people did, or what roles you played.

C: Write a concluding sentence that tells how teamwork made the event a success.

Now choose a partner. Exchange the first drafts of your reports. Each of you will write helpful comments on the other's report. Base your comments on the guidelines (A, B, and C) above. Use a chart like this one for your comments:

Title	Author	Opening Sentence	Description of Event	Concluding Sentence

Use your partner's comments to help you improve your final draft!

This story is about a community of monks who live together in their temple. Read on to discover if their household is a good example of teamwork.

Buddhism: a religion based on the wise sayings of Buddha, a teacher from India who lived in the sixth century, B.C. Buddha emphasized meditation and a moral way of life.

Three Monks, No Water

Story by TING-XING YE
Pictures by HARVEY CHAN

Once upon a time, there was a mountain; on that mountain, there stood a temple; and in that temple, all alone, lived a young monk.

Besides sweeping the temple, dusting the Buddha statues and replacing the burned incense sticks every day, the young monk would pray, meditate, and recite the scripture while beating rhythmically on a wooden block. It was a simple and peaceful life as he followed his vows in the service of Buddhism.

There was no water up in the temple, but there was a clear, cold stream at the foot of the mountain. Each morning, the young monk had to make his way down a narrow, winding trail to fetch water, carrying a shoulder pole with a wooden bucket dangling from each end. On the way down the mountain, the empty buckets danced left and right, right and left, in rhythm with his steps. But on the way back, the pole was bowed by the heavy buckets and it dug painfully into his shoulders.

Rain or shine, hot or cold, dry or damp, the young monk never missed a day lugging his burden up to the temple. With two buckets of water for drinking, cooking, and washing, he even had enough left over to start a vegetable garden. But how he wished someone else could help him someday!

One day the temple had a visitor. He was a middle-aged, tall and skinny monk, and his robe was sweaty and dusty from travelling. The young monk offered his tired guest fresh spring water and carefully cooked vegetables from the garden. After the meal, the young monk invited the skinny monk to stay in the temple and be company for him. His new companion accepted gracefully.

The next morning, when it was time to fetch water, they agreed that both of them should go down the mountain together. "That's only fair," they thought to themselves, "since we both will use the water."

But they soon discovered that the carrying-pole was too short to have two buckets placed in the middle while one of them shouldered each end, so they left one bucket behind. Nevertheless, on the way back to the temple they had to stop twice to adjust the bucket. It didn't matter whether the skinny monk was at the front or the back, the bucket would always slide down to the young monk's end and bang painfully against his legs.

"Ow! It hurts!" the young monk whined. "Why are you so cruel to me?"

"I didn't *try* to hurt you," the skinny monk snapped. "Can't you tell the problem is that I'm taller than you are? Don't blame me, blame gravity!"

At the third stop, with almost half of the water having slopped over the rim of the bucket, they marked the centre of the pole and placed the bucket on the line. With the young monk at the back, grabbing the bucket to stop it from sliding, they finally struggled into the temple. That day they had barely enough water for drinking and cooking and none for washing.

Instead of meditating that evening, they were both thinking the same thing: "Maybe tomorrow we will have enough water for the vegetable garden."

Long rainless days descended on the mountain; everything grew as dry as a bone. The two monks peered into the hot blue sky, licking their parched lips, wondering where the clouds had gone. In the garden the beans became scrawny and wrinkled. The green leaves of the cabbages turned yellow, and the tomato plants shrank into dry vines, hanging down helplessly along the wooden sticks. With one bucket of water a day, there were only a few drops left for the vegetables when the day ended.

"How could he be so unreasonable?" The skinny monk peeped at the young one, shaking his head. "He invited me to be his companion and I accepted without hesitation. He doesn't seem to know how to show his gratitude to a person who is willing to sacrifice, especially his senior. He ought to be at the stream now, bringing fresh water up to the temple to show his respect and appreciation."

While passing the half-empty bucket on the way to their afternoon meditation, each threw an angry glance at the other. But not one word was said.

One afternoon, the temple had another visitor, a big fat monk, carrying a case full of books. When he was offered a drink, he helped himself to two full bowls. After the meal, he asked his two new friends if he could be of help in the temple and be company for them. The young and the skinny monks stared at each other for a moment, then silently nodded their heads.

While they were beating wooden blocks and chanting scriptures that night, all three of them were thinking to themselves.

"I don't need to carry water any more," the young monk thought with full certainty. "I am younger than both of them, not to mention the fact that they are newcomers. They'd better not forget that taking care of a youngster is one of their commitments. Now, finally, my wish comes true." He almost burst into a smile.

"I bet my water-fetching days are over," the skinny monk thought confidently, with a grin on his face. "Clearly I am not as strong as they are because I am the eldest. Besides, since both of them are almost the same height, no one has to grab the bucket to keep it from sliding along the pole."

"Why should I break their daily routine?" the fat monk assured himself. "They know the path and are very skilled in carrying water. But most importantly, I am a scholar and full of knowledge. Everyone knows a scholar is not expected to do any physical labour." He confirmed his thought with a firm nod.

The next day, the sun rose and set, but the buckets remained empty. All three monks sat in the hall for the whole day, chanting and reciting and waiting for the others to make a move. But no one did. They shared the last gourd of water—saved from the previous day—before they went to bed. Each of them was saying the same thing to himself: "Tomorrow, those two *must* go down the mountain to get water!"

A day passed. No water. A second day went by. No water.

Nobody was out of bed when the fourth day arrived. The hall was deadly quiet, and so was the temple. No chanting, no beating rhythms on the wooden blocks.

In the silent temple, a little mouse popped his head from under the drapery that covered the incense table, looking around for food. With his tiny head tilted first to one side and then the other, he listened, and then he crawled up on the drapery. As he pulled himself up onto the tabletop, he bumped into a dish holding burning incense sticks, scattering them across the table and onto the floor. As the frightened mouse leapt from the table and scampered away, the draperies burst into flame, and soon the hall was full of smoke.

"Fire! Fire! Fire!" clamoured the young monk, running this way and that in panic.

"Help! Help! Help!" cried the skinny monk at the top of his lungs.

"The buckets! The buckets! Quick!" shouted the fat monk, pointing with both hands.

"Water!" yelled all three of them in unison.

But all the buckets were upside down, empty and dry.

The young monk grabbed the shoulder pole and two buckets and dashed to the mountain path. The skinny and the fat monks rushed into the hall. Choking and coughing, they peered through a sea of black smoke and saw the table blazing. Frantically, they stamped out the fire and dragged the smoking draperies out of the temple. As they hauled out the last one, a stubborn flame came to life again under the table.

At that moment the young monk appeared, totally out of breath, his shouldered pole bowed by two buckets of water. Quickly, he poured the water onto the flame and rushed back to the stream. When he returned a second time, the skinny monk took over the shoulder pole, adjusted the buckets and disappeared down the path.

At the end of the day, the exhausted monks couldn't remember how many buckets of water they had hauled up the mountain.

That night, in the smoke-damaged hall, together, they made a decision.

Early next morning, the three monks went down the mountainside and brought back a water vat. They installed it outside the temple. Carrying two buckets on his shoulder pole, the skinny monk scooted down and up the mountain to fill the vat with fresh water. The fat monk worked in the hall, moving out the smoke-damaged furniture, cleaning and fixing it.

And the young monk was totally absorbed in attending to the garden, straightening up the vegetables that had survived his neglect and planting some new ones. He made sure that each of them had more than enough to drink. "It's a treat from us," he said loudly to the vegetables, "not just for today, but every day from now on."

A week later, when the three monks gathered at the brimming vat and drank fresh water, they looked at the garden, where the weeds had poked their green leaves out between the rows of vegetables.

The young monk slowly stood up and headed towards the garden. His two friends were close behind. ◉

Afterword

When I was a kid, every time my brothers and sisters and I tried to find excuses for not doing household chores, or passed a work assignment to one another like a relay baton, my mother would always say, "It's typical. Three monks, no water." Years later, I learned that it was an old, widely used expression, with an unknown origin.

— Ting-xing Ye

FOLLOW UP

How did the monks come to understand the principles of teamwork? Do you think this story is meant to amuse us, to teach us a lesson, or both?

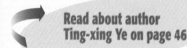

Read about author Ting-xing Ye on page 46

Something To Think About

Some people have reasons for what they do. Others have excuses. What is the difference between a reason and an excuse?

Understanding the Story

Fire! Help! Water!

- What chores did the young monk have to do every day when he was alone?

- What problems did the skinny monk and the young monk have when they tried to fetch water together?

- All three monks thought they had good reasons for not carrying water. Were they good reasons? Explain your opinion.

- What emergency took place in the temple? Did the three monks use teamwork to deal with it?

- At the end of the story the garden needs weeding. Who will help with this chore? What does this tell us about the lesson the monks have learned?

The Trouble with Teamwork

CLASS DISCUSSION

Trying to work together as a team can cause lots of problems. As the author showed, jealousy, complaints, and laziness all sabotage team efforts. As a class, talk about problems you've experienced trying to work in teams or groups. Then discuss solutions for these problems. After the discussion, a couple of volunteers could list ways to avoid problems. Turn it into a booklet called *Our Rule Book for Teamwork!*

YOUR TURN TO WRITE

A Co-operative Story

Try writing a story with several authors—either members of a small group or the whole class. Use the chalkboard to write down your ideas. Here's one way to go about it. Invent

- three characters
- a problem to be solved
- a funny incident or two
- an emergency
- a solution involving teamwork

When you're ready to write the story, choose one writer to create a first draft. The other students can suggest changes, but everyone has to agree on them. As you can see, this task involves co-operation skills. It can be lots of fun! Ask someone to illustrate the final version of your story.

Did You Know ?

Buddhist monks in China have helped people over the centuries—setting up hospitals, aiding the poor, and distributing food in times of famine. One of the greatest contributions of Buddhism was the invention of printing in the eighth century.

MEET AUTHOR

Ting-xing Ye

by Susan Hughes

When Ting-xing Ye [Ting-sing YAY] was a little girl in Shanghai, China, in the 1950s, there was never enough money for her family to buy books. If she had a spare coin, Ting-xing would take it to the street vendor. He would hand her a small book and watch her carefully as she sat on the curb to read it. When she was done, she had to give it back.

She loved books so much that she would read anything she could borrow. After she finished reading her own schoolbooks, she would gobble up her older brother's books.

Ting-xing grew up in China, but she didn't become a writer there. It was simply too dangerous. At that time, people were put in prison for expressing thoughts or ideas that the government did not approve of.

Ting-xing moved to Canada in 1987 to study at a university in Toronto.

"There were many things that I found amazing about this country," Ting-xing says. "For example, before I came here I had never eaten any uncooked food." It fascinated her that people in Canada ate raw vegetables in their salad. "And, of course, there were the big highways, all the cars—and lots more!"

Five years later, she moved to Orillia, Ontario, with her husband, successful children's book author, William Bell. Feeling shy about writing with her husband around, she waited until he went out of town for a few days—and that's when she first began to write! *Three Monks, No Water* was the result of her first creative attempt.

The story is based on an old Chinese poem that Ting-xing's mother often said to her. Translated, it goes like this:

> "One monk, two buckets.
> Two monks, one bucket.
> Three monks, no water."

Years later, far from China, Ting-xing sat down at her word processor and thought, "Why not try to turn that old expression into a story?" It became an imaginative tale about teamwork, and a successful picture book.

Shortly after this, Ting-xing began writing a memoir about her difficult years in China. "For a while, reliving painful memories made me feel miserable," she says. "I needed to write something cheerful."

That's why she wrote her second picture book set in China, *Weighing the*

Elephant. Like *Three Monks, No Water,* this story was sparked by someone else's words —in this case, her school math teacher. While teaching the class ways to measure things that are too big to weigh on a scale, he had used the example of an elephant.

"In this case, I knew the ending—how the little boy would weigh the elephant— so I had to work backwards and build the story from the beginning!" she laughs.

In her third story, *Fei-fei and the Kite,* Ting-xing changes course. It's about a young girl who moves from a small village in China to join her parents in North America. "In this story, I have Fei-fei experience the same amazing things as I did when I arrived," she says.

Ting-xing feels that writing *Fei-fei and the Kite* was a means of finally arriving in North America herself—of finishing one chapter of her life, and beginning a new one.

MORE GOOD READING

❧ *Prairie Fire!*
by Bill Freeman
The year is 1876. Jamie, Meg, and Kate Bains travel to Manitoba with their mother to claim free land for a homestead. The family is excited about finally owning their own farm, but they soon discover they have to work together to deal with fires and conflicts to settle their new home. (a novel)

❧ *Superstars on Ice*
by Patty Cranston
Want to find out more about what it takes to be a champion figure skater? This book offers action-filled photographs and lots of information about skating legends and today's hottest skaters, including singles, pairs, and ice dancers. (a non-fiction book)

Opening Days: Sports Poems
selected by
Lee Bennett Hopkins
Sports is all about movement, rhythm, teamwork. In this book you'll find a collection of eighteen poems about sports such as baseball, basketball, karate, and skiing. (a poetry book)

❧ *A People Apart*
by Catherine Kenna
Barn Raising showed you one glimpse of the way of life for Old Order Mennonites. This book is filled with beautiful black-and-white photographs that give you many portraits of how Mennonites work, farm, attend school, and play. (a photo-information book)

Send A MESSAGE

TELEPHONE TALK

Poem by **X. J. Kennedy**

Back flat on the carpet,
Cushion under my head,
Sock feet on the wallpaper,
Munching raisin bread,

Making easy whispers
Balance on high wire,
Trading jokes and laughing,
The two of us conspire,

Closer than when walking
Down the street together,
Closer than two sparrows
Hiding from wet weather.

How would my shrill whistle
Sound to you, I wonder?
Give a blow in your phone,
My phone makes it thunder.

Through the night, invisibly
Jumping over space,
Back and forth between us
All our secrets race.

Personal Response

- When you speak with your friends on the telephone, how do you make yourself comfortable?
- X. J. Kennedy paints vivid word pictures in this poem. Which picture is your favourite?
- Do you think it is easier to share secrets on the telephone than in person? Why, or why not?
- Some kids don't talk endlessly on the telephone. Think of three reasons why they might not do so.

A Telephone Conversation

Imagine that you are listening to a telephone conversation between two best friends. Write out their conversation. You will need to

- place the words each person says in quotation marks
- include a speech tag ("he said" or "asked Judy") for each speech
- indent the line for each new speaker

Here is an example:

"Guess what?" asked Judy.

"I don't know. You always make me guess. Maybe it's your birthday," said Abby.

"Wrong the first time. Guess again," Judy said.

"No way," said Abby. She sounded irritated.

Illustrate a Telephone Talk

Draw or paint a picture of yourself comfortably talking on the telephone.

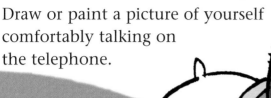

Did You Know

There are more than 525 million telephones in the world and they carry more than 400 billion conversations each year.

The United States has more phones than any other country: 120 million.

Tokyo, Japan, is the city with the most telephones in the world: 5 511 000.

Mother's Day is the busiest day of the year for telephone calls.

By the year 2000, experts estimate there will be 2.5 billion telephones in the world, and they'll carry a total of 2 quadrillion—that's 2 000 000 000 000 000—calls each year!

POET'S CRAFT

Rhythm & Rhyme

Telephone Talk has a regular beat (rhythm) and a regular rhyming pattern. With a partner, try reading it aloud.

- Decide how many beats there are in each line.

- Find the rhyming words in each four-line verse. Which pair of rhymes is your favourite?

- Think up one or two more words that rhyme with **head, wire, together, wonder,** and **space.** Which word was the hardest to rhyme?

Responding Activities **51**

BEFORE READING

●

Think of a time before the telephone or e-mail existed. How do you think people communicated with each other back then? Talk about it with a partner.

ARTICLE BY
Elizabeth MacLeod

PICTURES BY
Bill Slavin

Before Telephones

Suppose you were a cave person living thousands of years ago. As you're lounging in your cave entrance one day, you spot a herd of woolly mammoths thundering toward you. Yikes! You have to warn your cousin Gronk, who lives twenty caves over. But how? You could send your brother Blog running over with the message. (Nobody can write yet, so Blog better have a good memory.) Blog's busy? Get out the drums or send a smoke signal. Definitely low tech.

If you lived a little later, say about 3500 B.C., when people knew how to write, you wouldn't have to depend on Blog's memory, so you could send a longer message. You wouldn't have to depend on his feet either: you could send the message by horse, sailing ship, or homing pigeon. If you lived in Persia, your message could be shouted from one tower to the next by men with powerful voices—and good lungs!

20 000 B.C. Prehistoric people pass along news from person to person.

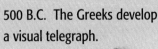
500 B.C. The Greeks develop a visual telegraph.

3500 B.C. First written language appears.

1793 Claude Chappé invents a signalling system.

52

Too slow? The Greeks thought so too, so around 500 B.C. they developed a visual telegraph. They built a series of brick walls just close enough together to see from one wall to the next. Indentations along the top of the wall represented each letter of the alphabet. To send your message, you lit fires in the correct indents. Someone on the next wall would see the fires and relay your message.

Later, books and daily news sheets made exchanging information easier. However, even as late as the eighteenth century, news still moved no faster than people on horseback or shipboard. Mail service made sending messages easier and cheaper, but not faster.

It wasn't until the late 1700s that French engineer Claude Chappé really sped up long-distance communication. He created a "telegraph" similar to the one back in Greece. Towers were built between Paris and other major cities in France, each topped by a huge crossbar with two arms. An operator moved the crossbar and arms to spell out a message, which was read through a telescope by the operator in the next tower. Messages were passed along from tower to tower at the lightning speed of 120 km per minute. By the mid-1800s, most of Europe used Chappé's system.

Around 1816, you could communicate using flags of various colours and patterns in different positions. This system could transmit eight thousand symbols. Not only were there too many to remember, but the code book was constantly being changed. Despite its problems, this system was useful for ships trying to talk to nearby ships.

On land, steam-powered trains transported messages round the world faster than horses could manage. Still not fast enough? By the mid-1700s, scientists were working on transmitting electric signals. These were instant—but experts didn't have a way to control them and use them to transmit information. Then along came Samuel F. B. Morse with an electric telegraph system that worked. Finally you could warn Gronk instantly of danger. Only one problem—woolly mammoths had been extinct for centuries.

1816 Ships use flag-signalling systems.

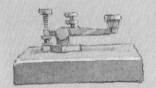
1844 Morse invents the electric telegraph.

1866 A telegraph cable links Europe and North America.

1876 Alexander Graham Bell invents the telephone.

FOLLOW UP

Which forms of communication were new to you? Which ones do we still use today?

Understanding the Article

Messages from the Past

- How do you think cave people used drums or smoke signals to send messages?

- How did writing make it easier to send messages?

- Outline how the Greeks' visual telegraph worked.

- How was Claude Chappé's telegraph similar to the Greek system? In what ways was it an improvement?

- What was the biggest advantage of the electric telegraph system?

Make a Personal Time Line

Make a horizontal line on a large piece of paper. At intervals, write a number for each year of your age. Then for each year, write an important event that might have held a message for you. It could be a message about life, about people, a special event, or something you learned at school. Illustrate your time line.

My baby brother arrives.

I write my first story in class.

Time Line

| Age | 1 | 2 | 3 | 4 | 5 | 6 | 7 | 8 |

A Story

For communication to take place you need a sender, a message, and a receiver. Choose one of the time periods in the article's time line. Invent (1) a person who wants to send a message, (2) the message itself, and (3) the person who should receive the message. Then tell a funny story about what happens when the sender tries to send that message.

IMAGINE!

All the telephones in the world disappear.
How will your life be different?

Lindy, my dog, is my birthday surprise.

9   10   11   12

Did You Know?

Samuel F.B. Morse invented the first reliable electric telegraph machine. By tapping a key, the operator caused a pencil to make long or short marks on a strip of paper. These dots and dashes made sense if you knew the Morse code — another of his inventions. Here are some examples:

The alphabet

A . —

B — . . .

C — . — .

(and on to Z)

The distress signal

SOS . . . — — — . . .

Research Project

Find out about Alexander Graham Bell and how he invented the telephone.

Make notes from library books and/or the Internet. Present your findings in the form of a time line with dates, pictures, and a sentence or two for each item.

What do you know about slaves in the southern United States, 150 years ago? Read this story to find out about one young girl's clever plan to escape from the South to the North.

Sweet Clara and the Freedom Quilt

Story by DEBORAH HOPKINSON   Pictures by JAMES RANSOME

Before I was even twelve years old, I got sent from North Farm to Home Plantation 'cause they needed another field hand. When I got there, I cried so much they thought I was never gon' eat or drink again. I didn't want to leave my momma.

"I'm goin' back to her," I whispered every day to Young Jack, who worked beside me in the fields.

"Well, you better start eatin' all you can, Sweet Clara." He
smiled at me. But then his smile was gone. In a low voice he say,
"Or else you won't make it."

Young Jack helped me believe I'd get back to my momma
someday. Truth was, I'd be lost before I got through the fields,
them being so big and all. But I didn't give up dreamin'.

Aunt Rachel was raising me now. She wasn't my for-real blood
aunt, but she did her best to care for me.

One night she come back from working in the Big House and
found me lying dead tired on our cabin floor. She shook her
head and say, "Sweet Clara, you aine gon' last in the fields. But I
got an idea."

Aunt Rachel's idea was sewin'—and she started teachin' me
the very next night. It wasn't easy for me to learn, my hands
already rough and clumsy from hoeing and weeding the fields.
So Aunt Rachel took it real slow.

She brought scraps of cloth from the Big House and taught
me 'bout each one, how it was special and had to be treated in
its own way. I liked to piece the scraps together to make pretty
patterns of colours. But Aunt Rachel didn't care much about
pretty patterns.

"Now you rip out that whole row and do it again, Clara,"
she say.

"Why I got to make the stitches so tiny?" I complained.

"You gon' be a real *seamstress,* that's why."

"Tomorrow you comin' with me to the Big House. I got it all worked out," Aunt Rachel say one day.

I was frightened.

"You ready to sew with me," she went on. "Missus' daughter Ella be gettin' married come spring. I told Missus I'd be needin' help. She look at yo' work with sharp eyes, Clara, so do it quick and neat like I taught you."

Next morning I tried to eat some corn bread, but my insides was all knotted up. I never been inside the Big House before or seen white people that close—'cept the overseer.

The morning sun was streamin' into the sewin' room, turning everything all sunflower yellow. Aunt Rachel give me some sheets to hem. Instead of being contrary, that needle did all I wanted, just like it was part of my hand.

At the end of the day, Missus come in. "Let me see your work, Clara," she say.

I gave her the sheet, and she ran it through her hands real slow. I held my breath, watching.

"From now on, come here," she say at last.

When she left, Aunt Rachel and I looked at each other, about ready to burst. "We done it, girl!" she cried.

So I changed from a field hand to a seamstress. Since the sewin' room was right off the kitchen, Aunt Rachel and I were near Cook and the helpers. There was always lots of bustle and company in the kitchen. I was hearing about all kinds of new places and things. I listened so hard it felt like my ears must be growing right out of my head and gettin' big with listening.

One day two white men come to see the master. The drivers went into the kitchen to talk to Cook.

"There been too many runaways last summer," one of the drivers said. "They goin' round askin' all the masters in the county to join the patrollers."

"Crazy, runnin' away," muttered Cook as she beat up some batter. "Where you gon' get to 'cept lost in the swamp?"

"Dunno," said the other. "But I hear we aine that far from the Ohio River. Once you get that far, the Underground Railroad will carry you across."

"That's right," agreed the first. "The Railroad will get you all the way to Canada. Then you free forever."

Cook snorted. "If it be as easy as you two let on, more woulda gone."

One of the men replied in a quiet voice, "It be easy if you could get a map."

Walking back from the Big House that evening I asked Aunt Rachel 'bout what I'd heard. "Where's Canada? And what's the Underground Railroad?"

"See there?" Aunt Rachel pointed. "That's the North Star. Under that star, far up north, is Canada. The Underground Railroad is people who been helpin' folks get there, secret-like."

She looked at me hard. "But don't you start thinkin' 'bout it. You run away and get caught, you be beaten."

Still, I couldn't *stop* thinking about it. Next day I asked Cook, "Those two men that was here yesterday. They was talking 'bout a map. What's a map?"

"Just a picture of the land, that's all. Whatever's on the ground, a map can have it."

Sunday I went to my favourite place on the little hill and looked out at the people's cabins and the fields. I took a stick and started making a picture in the dirt of all I could see.

But how could I make a picture of things far away that I *couldn't* see? And how could I make a map that wouldn't be washed away by the rain—a map that would show the way to freedom?

Then one day I was sewin' a patch on a pretty blue blanket. The patch looked just the same shape as the cow pond near the cabins. The little stitches looked like a path going all round it. Here it was—a picture that wouldn't wash away. A map!

So I started the quilt.

When you sewin', no matter how careful you be, little scraps of cloth always be left after you cut out a dress or a pillowcase. So while my ears kept listening, and my hands kept sewin', I began to squirrel away these bits of cloth.

When we was off work, I went to visit people in the Quarters. I started askin' what fields was where. Then I started piecin' the scraps of cloth with the scraps of things I was learnin'.

Aunt Rachel say, "Sweet Clara, what kind of pattern you makin' in that quilt? Aine no pattern I ever seen."

"I don't know, Aunt Rachel. I'm just patchin' it together as I go." She looked at me long, but she just nodded.

There was a buzzing in the Quarters one summer evening. I saw the patrollers and I knew someone had run away. It was Young Jack. But five days later they caught him.

That next Sunday I went to see him, and we walked to the top of the little hill. He didn't smile the way he used to.

I took a stick and began to draw in the dirt. I drew a little square for Big House, a line of boxes for the cabins of the Quarters, and some bigger squares for the fields east of Big House. I drew as much as I'd pieced together.

Jack sat beside me, not sayin' anything. Not even looking at first. Then he started seeing what I was doing. I handed the stick to him. I hear him catch his breath up quick. Then he begun to draw.

I worked on the quilt for a long time. Sometimes months would go by and I wouldn't get any pieces sewn in it. Sometimes I had to wait to get the right kind of cloth— I had blue calico and flowered blue silk for creeks and rivers, and greens and blue-greens for the fields, and white sheeting for roads. Missus liked to wear pink a lot, so Big House, the Quarters, and finally, the Big House at North Farm, they was all pink.

The quilt got bigger and bigger, and if folks knew what I was doin', no one said. But they came by the sewin' room to pass the time of day whenever they could.

"By the way, Clara," a driver might tell me, "I heard the master sayin' yesterday he didn't want to travel to Mr. Morse's place 'cause it's over twenty miles north o' here."

Or someone would sit eatin' Cook's food and say, so as I could hear, "Word is they gon' plant corn in the three west fields on the Verona plantation this year."

When the master went out huntin', Cook's husband was the guide. He come back and say, "That swamp next to Home Plantation is a nasty place. But listen up, Clara, and I'll tell you how I thread my way in and out of there as smooth as yo' needle in that cloth."

Then one night the quilt was done. I looked at it spread out in the dim light of the cabin. Aunt Rachel studied it for the longest time. She touched the stitches lightly, her fingers moving slowly over the last piece I'd added—a hidden boat that would carry us across the Ohio River. Finally, they came to rest on the bright star at the top.

She tried to make her voice cheery. "You always did like to make patterns and pictures, Clara. You get yourself married to Young Jack one of these days, and you two will have a real nice quilt to sleep under."

"Aunt Rachel, I couldn't sleep under this quilt," I answered softly, putting my hand over hers. "Wouldn't be restful, somehow. Anyway, I think it should stay here. Maybe others can use it."

Aunt Rachel sighed. "But aine you gon' need the quilt where you goin'?"

I kissed her. "Don't worry, Aunt Rachel. I got the memory of it in my head."

It rained hard for three days the next week. Me and Jack left Home Plantation in a dark thunderstorm. The day after, it was too stormy to work in the fields, so Jack wasn't missed. And Aunt Rachel told them I was sick.

We went north, following the trail of the freedom quilt. All the things people told me about, all the tiny stitches I took, now I could see real things. There was the old tree struck down by lightning, the winding road near the creek, the hunting path through the swamp. It was like being in a dream you already dreamed.

Mostly we hid during the day and walked at night. When we got to North Farm, Jack slipped in through the darkness to find what cabin my momma at. Then we went in to get her and found a little sister I didn't even know I had. Momma was so surprised.

"Sweet Clara! You growed so big!" Her eyes just like I remembered, her arms strong around me.

"Momma, I'm here for you. We goin' North. We know the way."

I was afraid they wouldn't come. But then Momma say yes. Young Jack carried my sister Anna, and I held on to Momma's hand.

We kept on as fast as we could, skirting farms and towns and making our way through the woods. At last, one clear dark night, we come to the Ohio River. The river was high, but I remembered the place on the quilt where I'd marked the crossing. We searched the brush along the banks until at last we found the little boat.

"This was hid here by the folks in the Underground Railroad," I said.

The boat carried us across the dark, deep water to the other side. Shivering and hungry and scared, we stood looking ahead.

"Which way now?" Jack asked me.

I pointed. The North Star was shining clear above us. "Up there through the woods. North. To Canada."

Sometimes I think back to the night we left, when Young Jack come to me. I can still see Aunt Rachel sitting up in her bed. She just shook her head before I could say a word.

"Before you go, just cover me with your quilt, Sweet Clara," she say. "I'm too old to walk, but not too old to dream. And maybe I can help others follow the quilt to freedom."

Aunt Rachel kept her word. The quilt is there still, at Home Plantation. People go look at it, even folks from neighbouring farms. I know because some of them come and tell me how they used it to get free. But not all are as lucky as we were, and most never can come.

Sometimes I wish I could sew a quilt that would spread over the whole land, and the people just follow the stitches to freedom, as easy as taking a Sunday walk. 🔹

What new things did you learn about slavery in this story? What did you find most interesting about Clara's escape plan?

Understanding the Story

Message in a Quilt

- What did Clara hope for at the beginning of the story?

- How did Aunt Rachel help Clara to take the first step toward freedom?

- Why did Clara think of making a quilt that was also a map?

- How did she piece her quilt-map together?

- Why did Clara leave the quilt behind when she and Jack ran away?

- Who did Clara take with her on her escape route?

- Where did Clara and the other runaways go to find freedom?

- Why was Clara's quilt a good way to leave a message for others who might want to escape?

Viewing the Illustrations

There's a saying that a picture is worth a thousand words. What can you discover from the illustrations in this story?

- What kinds of clothing did men, women, and girls wear 150 years ago?

- What kind of cabins did Aunt Rachel and the other slaves live in?

- What was the countryside like around the Plantation?

Design a Quilt with a Message

IMAGINE!

You meet Clara when she arrives in Canada. Write a story about your adventures together.

Clara's quilt had a unique message. Many traditional quilt designs have special meanings, too.

A turkey tracks quilt.

- **Turkey Tracks:** Some people believed that a child who slept under a quilt with this design would grow up to become a wanderer.

- **Album:** When a woman moved away, friends and neighbours would each sew a block of fabric on a quilt. That way, the woman would always remember those left behind.

- **Military:** These quilts were made from scraps of old uniforms. Sometimes they were sewn by captured soldiers during the American Civil War.

A crazy quilt.

- **Crazy:** Some quilters liked to use random-sized pieces of extravagant fabric, like velvets and silks. They sewed them together with big, fancy stitches.

Design your own small quilt with a message. Make a drawing of your design. If you can get some help, cut out fabric pieces and sew them together to make your quilt.

Did You Know ?

The Underground Railroad was neither underground nor a railroad. But the name helped to provide a cover for the runaway slaves and their helpers. Railroad terms were used as a secret code: escape routes were called "lines," stopping places were called "stations," helpers were "conductors," and the escaping slaves were called "packages" or "freight." Spirituals, the religious songs of the slaves, also contained secret messages that helped runaways escape to freedom.

Do you and your friends share special words that your parents don't use? Many groups — such as doctors and hockey players — have special expressions. This article reveals some of the "lingo" cowboys favour.

Article by
LINDA
GRANFIELD

Pictures by
SETH

Cowboyspeak

A cowboy's language was a colourful mix of words and expressions. The language reflected the many cultures found in any group of cowhands: Mexican, French, British, Jewish, Native, Métis, and African American.

Writers in the 1920s collected some of the cowboy vocabulary. Imaginative novelists made up other words as they wrote their books, and claimed the lingo was "gen-u-ine." What we call **cowboyspeak** is a blend of documented and invented words and expressions, kept alive and embroidered in today's western movies and books.

Here's a typical conversation between a couple of cowhands, sitting around a campfire as they might have done over one hundred years ago.

Pardner, that tenderfoot will larn. He'll amble into the bunkhouse and find his wish book missin'. If his scabbards is missin', too, he'll be spooked all right.

It's time to hit the trail. When it's done, this child will be as happy as a little dog with two tails.

Translation:

A. Well, Slim, I'm getting a little fed up. I'm sick of eating beans every day. Pass the coffee, will you?

B. I agree with you, buddy. I'd like some canned fruit on the next drive. Some milk would taste pretty good, too. Did you hear Dutch last night? He wouldn't stop talking about his firearms. I plan to stick a prairie dog in his bunk the next time he does that. I was tired, and he kept going on about them.

A. That newcomer will learn, pal. He'll walk into the bunkhouse and find his mail-order catalogue missing. If his holsters are missing, too, he'll be pretty scared.

B. It's time to get to work. Boy, will I be happy when this drive is over!

A Cowgirl Today

Jessica Chalmers is thirteen years old, and she has lived on ranches all her life. She represents the fourth generation of her family to live on the Chalmers Ranch in Millarville, Alberta. The ranch once covered twelve hundred hectares in the foothills near Calgary, but has been divided and is now smaller.

Jessica's grandparents, who still live on the original ranch, now have about two hundred head of cattle, which her cowboy father, Doug, helps herd.

It's spring, and Jessica shares her story of life on a ranch:

"I've been riding horses since I could barely sit up on one. By the time I was three, I was riding around my grandparents' ranch. Now I like to ride my grandfather's horse, Jack. He's a big quarter horse, chestnut-coloured and seventeen hands high. I've been lucky. I've never gotten sore from riding, even after chasing cattle or riding a long time. The best thing about living on a ranch is that you can go riding whenever you want!

"All of my friends live on ranches, but we go to school in Calgary. I'm in grade seven. I want to be a veterinarian when I'm older. You can't just ranch now. You have to go to university, get a degree, *and* ranch. Veterinarians can travel and work on many ranches. They can help the cows when they have problems with their calves.

"The cattle on the ranch are purebred Salers. It's calving time now. There'll be about a hundred calves. Sometimes I have a favourite. Like Gracie. Her mother stepped on her after she was born, and I took care of her.

"When I was about nine years old, I helped out on my first roundup. We woke up about four o'clock in the morning and worked until noon. Then we ate lunch on the side of the road; my grandmother makes the best chili in the world! Then back to work all afternoon. Because the roundup was near the ranch, I could go home at night and sleep in my soft bed instead of on the ground.

"When people ask what's the worst part about living on a ranch, I say there's *no* worst part. My friends and I go riding together a lot, and have even visited dude ranches with some of our friends who live in Calgary. It's funny to watch the city riders at the dude ranches. They just want to run, run, run. They race around on their horses, and don't like to just trot.

"City kids are sometimes surprised when they visit our ranch. Ranch kids sometimes wear cowboy hats, but not all the time. And I only wear cowboy boots for protection when I'm going to ride. I don't wear spurs when I ride, because if you have a good horse you don't need them. When I'm not riding, I like to play the saxophone and watch the latest *Star Trek* television shows— not the old ones! And I'd like to be a pilot like my mother. Maybe I'll be a flying veterinarian!" ⬡

FOLLOW UP

Have you heard any of these cowboy expressions – either in real life or in western movies? Which of them were new to you? Which of them have become part of your everyday language?

Personal Response

- Have you ever wished you could be a cowboy or a cowgirl?
- What is your favourite western movie?
- What do you know about modern cowboys in Canada and the United States?
- What did you find most interesting about Jessica Chalmers' life on an Alberta ranch?

An Alberta cowboy in the 1880s.

A family cattle drive.

Understanding the Selection

Lasso That Lingo!

- North American cowboys were a multicultural group. What are some of the cultures they came from?

- Why do you think cowhands developed their own lingo?

- Linda Granfield writes, "Cowboyspeak is a blend of **documented** and **invented** words and expressions." What do these two words mean? Find synonyms (words that mean the same) for them in your dictionary.

IMAGINE!

Nowadays cowgirls work right along with male cowboys. Invent some "Cowgirlspeak" that reflects their pride and skill!

Act It Out!

What happens when Slim puts a prairie dog in Dutch's bunk to teach him a lesson? Make up a scene for two or three actors, using Cowboyspeak for the dialogue. You can invent any new words and phrases you need. When you have rehearsed your scene, present it to the class.

TIPS for Actors:

Volume – Speak loudly and clearly enough for everyone to hear you.

Gesture – Choose movements and hand gestures that make your meaning clear.

A modern cowboy.

Create a Cowboyspeak Dictionary

Reread the conversation between the two cowboys. Then read the translation of the conversation. In your notebook, make a column of Cowboyspeak words and phrases (there are about twenty) in alphabetical order. Beside each entry, write the definition. Now illustrate your dictionary of Cowboyspeak!

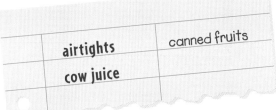

airtights	canned fruits
cow juice	

TECH LINK
A multimedia design tool would provide an interesting way of presenting your work.

Jimmy Jet
AND His TV Set

Poem and illustrations by
Shel Silverstein

I'll tell you the story of Jimmy Jet—
And you know what I tell you is true.
He loved to watch his TV set
Almost as much as you.

He watched all day, he watched all night
Till he grew pale and lean,
From "The Early Show" to"The Late Late Show"
And all the shows between.

He watched till his eyes were frozen wide,
And his bottom grew into his chair.
And his chin turned into a tuning dial,
And antennae grew out of his hair.

And his brains turned into TV tubes,
And his face to a TV screen.
And two knobs saying "vert." and "horiz."
Grew where his ears had been.

And he grew a plug that looked like a tail
So we plugged in little Jim.
And now instead of him watching TV
We all sit around and watch him.

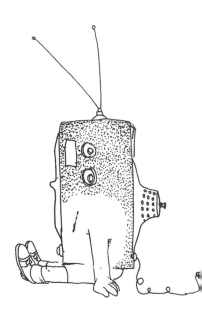

A Poem

What if you became a character in your favourite TV show or video game? Brainstorm some funny ideas about what happens to you. Then write a poem about your experience. If you wish, use four-line rhyming verses like Shel Silverstein's.

Word Pictures

Shel Silverstein is a master of humorous poetry. In this poem, the pictures he paints as Jimmy turns into a TV set are hilarious. What is the funniest word picture in the poem, in your opinion?

Something To Think About

Is it possible to watch too much television? What do you consider to be too much television? Why? If you were not watching TV, what other activities might you get involved in?

BEFORE READING

Think about some TV commercials you have seen. Which one do you like best, and why? Which one do you dislike the most? Why? Read the article to find out why there are so many commercials on TV.

Text by
Shelagh Wallace

Media SPOTLIGHT

"We'll Be Right Back After These Messages"

You're watching your favourite show, it's just getting to a really good part and then...a commercial. What do you do? Go to the kitchen? Press the mute button? Watch the commercial?

If you're an average TV viewer, you'll find yourself in this situation many, many times. During a year, you see (or perhaps choose not to see) at least 20 000 commercials. Commercials pay for most of the programs you watch. TV networks charge advertisers to air the ads, then use the money they receive to cover the costs of producing the shows.

TV TIDBIT

Advertisers often spend more creating a commercial that lasts one minute than TV producers spend making a half-hour show. Between 20 and 40 percent of a product's price goes to pay for the cost of advertising it, including its commercials. So if you buy a toy that costs $29.95, between $6 and $12 of your money goes to telling you and others about it!

SOME TV TRICKS OF THE TRADE

Advertisers use special techniques to get your attention and hold it for the entire length of the commercial. Here are just some of those techniques:

- **Repeating the ad over and over again.** Studies show that many people are more likely to buy an advertised brand instead of an unadvertised brand, even if the unadvertised brand is cheaper. One reason you're familiar with the advertised brand name is that you've heard the ad for it over and over again.

- **Using camera effects and special effects.** Close-ups can make products look larger than they are. Computer-generated special effects can make toys appear to do something, such as move by themselves. They won't actually do that when you get them home.

- **Emphasizing "premiums" (the toys or prizes that come with certain products).** The "special gift inside" may be the only reason you buy the cereal.

- **Showing or saying words such as "free," "new," "amazing," and "improved" to get everyone's attention.** Did someone say "free"?

- **Hiring famous people to tell you to buy a certain product (endorsements).** Advertisers conduct surveys to find out which celebrities you trust and like the most, then use those people to promote their products.

DON'T KID AROUND WITH KIDS!

The TV networks, governments, and advertisers agree that children are a special part of the TV audience. In Canada, the CRTC (Canadian Radio-Television and Telecommunications Commission) has hundreds of rules for advertisers.

Batteries not included

Advertisers are required to show or say "disclaimers," such as "batteries not included," in toy and cereal ads. Here's your chance to find out what advertisers are really saying when they use these phrases. Find the disclaimer in the left column, then look directly beside it, in the right column, for its meaning.

The Disclaimer Says:	What the Disclaimer Really Means:
"Some assembly required"	You have to put the toy together before it will work.
"Accessories sold separately"	All the great stuff you see in this commercial doesn't come with this toy.
"Batteries not included"	You must buy batteries and put them in the toy before it will work.
"Part of a complete breakfast"	If you eat this cereal with certain nutritious foods, such as milk, fruit, and toast, then you will have a completely nutritious breakfast.

Kids under five years of age don't understand that commercials are there to sell them something. To them, ads are just shorter programs. It isn't until kids are about eight years of age that they understand that commercials aren't always literally true. Because of this, the advertising industries in both Canada and the U.S. must obey special rules. These rules restrict what can be advertised to kids under twelve and how it can be advertised to them.

For example, the rules say advertisers can't take advantage of you by having a baseball player tell you how great a particular brand of bat is. He can endorse a sports drink, but not a bat or a baseball. What's the difference? Bats and baseballs are too close to what the player does for a living. Seeing him advertise either a bat or a baseball could leave you with the impression that you'll play like him if you buy one, too.

Another rule says computer-generated effects in commercials are okay, as long as there's at least one part of the ad that shows the product as it actually is. If a toy plane can't fly on its own, the ad has to show someone's hand holding the plane.

Two U.S. toy companies had to pay large fines when the Federal Trade Commission decided that their ads were misleading people. In one ad, a toy helicopter was made to look as if it could actually fly when it couldn't. In another ad, a ballerina doll was made to look as if it could stand and twirl all by itself without being held.

CALLING ALL SHOPPERS!

Why do advertisers bother trying to reach kids when there are so many restrictions on what advertisers can say and do on TV? Because kids are a very important, very profitable market.

In Canada, *TG Magazine*, a teen publication, estimates that Canadian teenagers spend a total of more than eighty million dollars a week. As well as spending their own money, kids influence what their families buy.

Even if you don't have any money to spend now, you will in a few years. You are the consumers of tomorrow. By aiming commercials at you now, advertisers are building "brand loyalty" (your loyalty or faithfulness for a particular brand or product). They hope this will pay off when you start spending in the years ahead. ⬡

TV ADVERTISERS' GLOSSARY

brand: a particular make of product, such as Nike or Kellogg's

celebrity: a person who is well-known and often in the news

consumer: shopper, a person who buys products

endorse: to recommend or approve a product

market: the consumers who might be persuaded to buy a product

network: a group of television stations that belong to the same company

product: something that is made to be bought by shoppers

promote: advertise

survey: a detailed study of people's opinions and buying habits

FOLLOW UP

In your notebook, list three new things you learned about TV commercials.

Something To Think About

Sometimes you watch an ad on TV without even knowing it's an ad. Some examples are:

• Saturday morning cartoons – they have popular characters that are also toys you can buy

• Music videos – they persuade you to buy the band's recordings and concert tickets

• Infomercials – these "information shows" look like real half-hour TV programs, but their only purpose is to sell a product

With a partner, discuss why you should be aware that commercial messages are all around you.

Understanding the Article

Got the Message?

• Why are there so many commercials on TV?

• Which of the "TV Tricks of the Trade" is the most convincing, in your opinion?

• Why does the government have rules about advertising to kids under twelve?

• Do you agree that young children should be protected from misleading ads?

• Why do ads sometimes need to have "disclaimers"?

• Do you think TV commercials could persuade you to buy a particular product? How can you become more "savvy" about the power of advertising?

IMAGINE!

Your ad agency has been hired to create a commercial for Pogo running shoes (or a product of your choice). You have come up with a great idea. Now you have to present it on paper. How will you do it?

Viewing Commercials

Ads for running shoes are carefully designed to get your attention and to convince you to buy one brand over all the others. TV advertisers use a variety of persuasion techniques. Three common techniques are:

1. **Testimonial** – A celebrity athlete tells us how well he/she runs or jumps in Pogo running shoes. If you wear them, you can be a good athlete, too!

2. **Bandwagoning** – The ad tells viewers that everybody is buying Pogo running shoes, so they must be good.

3. **Image Advertising** – The ad shows that people wearing Pogo running shoes are having a good time, so you'll have more fun and be more cool if you wear them, too.

Watch some commercials on TV. For each one, decide which persuasion technique it is using. If it's none of the above, make up a new name!

Birthday Box

STORY BY Jane Yolen   PICTURES BY Sylvie Daigneault

I was ten years old when my mother died. Ten years old on that very day. Still she gave me a party of sorts. Sick as she was, Mama had seen to it, organizing it at the hospital. She made sure the doctors and nurses all brought me presents. We were good friends with them all by that time, because Mama had been in the hospital for so long.

The head nurse, V. Louise Higgins (I never did know what that V stood for), gave me a little box, which was sort of funny because she was the biggest of all the nurses there. I mean she was tremendous. And she was the only one who insisted on wearing all white. Mama had called her the great white shark when she was first admitted, only not to V. Louise's face. "All those needles," Mama had said. "Like teeth." But V. Louise was sweet, not sharklike at all, and she'd been so gentle with Mama.

I opened the little present first. It was a fountain pen, a real one, not a fake one like you get at Kmart.

"Now you can write beautiful stories, Katie," V. Louise said to me.

I didn't say that stories come out of your head, not out of a pen. That wouldn't have been polite, and Mama— even sick—was real big on politeness.

"Thanks, V. Louise," I said.

The Stardust Twins—which is what Mama called Patty and Tracey-lynn because they reminded her of dancers in an old-fashioned ballroom—gave me a present together. It was a diary and had a picture of a little girl in pink, reading in a garden swing. A little young for me, a little too cute. I mean, I read Stephen King and want to write like him. But as Mama always reminded me whenever Dad finally remembered to send me something, it was the thought that counted, not the actual gift.

"It's great," I told them. "I'll write in it with my new pen." And I wrote my name on the first page just to show them I meant it.

They hugged me and winked at Mama. She tried to wink back but was just too tired and shut both her eyes instead.

Lily, who is from Jamaica, had baked me some sweet bread. Mary Margaret gave me a gold cross blessed by the Pope, which I put on even though Mama and I weren't churchgoers. That was Dad's thing.

Then Dr. Dann, the intern who was on days, and Dr. Pucci, the oncologist (which is the fancy name for a cancer doctor), gave me a big box filled to the top with little presents, each wrapped up individually. All things they knew I'd love— paperback books and writing paper and erasers with funny animal heads and coloured paper clips and a rubber stamp that printed FROM KATIE'S DESK and other stuff. They must have raided a stationery store.

There was one box, though, they held out till the end. It was about the size of a large top hat. The paper was deep blue and covered with stars; not fake stars but real stars, I mean, like a map of the night sky. The ribbon was two shades of blue with silver threads running through. There was no name on the card.

"Who's it from?" I asked.

None of the nurses answered, and the doctors both suddenly were studying the ceiling tiles with the kind of intensity they usually saved for X-rays. No one spoke. In fact the only sound for the longest time was Mama's breathing machine going in and out and in and out. It was a harsh, horrible, insistent sound, and usually I talked and talked to cover up the noise. But I was waiting for someone to tell me.

At last V. Louise said, "It's from your mama, Katie. She told us what she wanted. And where to get it."

FOLLOW UP

● How do you think Katie felt about losing her mother? How does her behaviour show how she is feeling? What happens to help her to start feeling better?

Fill a Story Box

Bring an empty shoe box from home and make it your story box. In it, put notes with ideas for stories you could write, characters you could create, and places you'd like to write about.

Add objects you find that might inspire you to write. Add poems and stories you have already written. Add photos, programs, tickets – anything that might spark a memory. Decorate your Story Box. The next time you can't think of anything to write, look through the box and you'll get lots of ideas!

Understanding the Story

A Box to Fill

- Why was Katie's mother in hospital?
- What did the hospital staff members give Katie for her birthday? Why did they choose these gifts?
- What did Katie's mother give her? What was strange about Mama's gift?

- A year after her mother died, Katie finally understood why Mama gave her an empty box, and why she said, "It's you." Explain why in your own words.
- What did Katie start doing when she finally understood her mother's message?

The Message Behind the Gift

Gifts often mean more than just what they are. For example, if you give someone a heart-shaped box of chocolates on Valentine's Day, you're sending a message, not just giving the person something to eat. What is the message? As you complete this chart in your notebook, add your own ideas about gifts with a message.

Gift	Recipient	Message
baseball glove	couch-potato friend	?
cookbook	father	?
set of paints	?	?
(add your ideas)		

MORE GOOD READING

☘ **Wild Talk: How Animals Talk to Each Other**
by Marilyn Baillie
Fireflies blink and cranes dance; bullfrogs croak and zebras neigh. Animals all over the world talk to each other in amazing ways. Read this book to discover why wolves and lemurs leave smelly signals, and why whales sing. (a science book)

☘ **Lights, Camera, Action: Making Movies and TV from the Inside Out**
by Lisa O'Brien
Have you ever wondered what goes on behind the scenes when a movie or TV show is being made? This book tells you how actors audition for parts, how directors control the action, how camera operators film it all—and much, much more. (a non-fiction book)

☘ **Cowboy: A Kid's Album**
by Linda Granfield
Everyone loves cowboy movies. But this book tells the *real* story behind the cowboys and cowgirls—free-spirited folk who made a livelihood herding cattle in the western wilderness. Don't miss the facts, fun, and great photos! (an information book)

☘ **Cybersurfer: The OWL Internet Guide for Kids**
by Nyla Ahmad
For a history of communications since the invention of television, this book is perfect. You'll learn how the Internet is creating new worldwide communities. And you'll find lists of great Web sites that will keep you busy for months. (a non-fiction book)

What's Fair?

ou for
r brother

You stand up for someone who is being picked on.

No matter how hard you study, you don't do well on your science test.

hour later.

You get a $1 a week raise in your allowance

Take a What's Fair? Card

It's Not Fair...

Personal Account by Jonathan Schwartz, age 10

IT'S NOT FAIR

1. ...when I raise my hand and keep my mouth shut and wait my turn, and the teacher calls on someone else.

2. ...when kids who won't co-operate wreck everyone else's good time.

3. ...if I save my allowance and want to buy something and my parents say I can't buy it because they don't think it's a good thing to buy.

4. ...when my older brother gets a later bedtime, just because he is older.

5. ...when you have a teacher who seems to like the girls better. Boys get in trouble for any little thing, but the girls never get spoken to.

6. ...when a kid trips me and doesn't get in trouble, but I do get in trouble for tripping him back.

7. ...when the same kids always get to be in charge of choosing the teams.

8. ...when kids get teased about something they can't help, like where they come from, or if they have something wrong with them.

Mom blar
something
has done.

You get to st

Your best friend is mad at you but won't tell you why.

Take a What's Fair? Card

Your favourite lunch is being served in the cafeteria.

Move ahead 3 squares

nally get to have
ol of the channel
er.

head 4 squares

Dad blames you for something you didn't do.

Move back 2 squares

DETENTION!

Miss a turn

87

Critical Response

- What is the most unfair thing on Jonathan Schwartz's list (page 87)?

- Do you think all the items on his list are unfair? List any that you think are fair after all.

- Does Jonathan always support his opinions with good reasons? Which of his opinions could use more support?

- Place each item in one of these categories: **Home, School,** or **Community.** Which categories have the most items?

Opinions with Reasons

YOUR TURN TO WRITE

Make your own list of opinions about five things that seem unfair. Then make another list of five things that you think are fair. For each opinion, give a good reason why you think this way.

"It's not fair because..."

"It is fair because..."

Try to choose at least two situations in each of these three categories: **Home, School,** and **Community**.

Role-Playing — Unfair Situations

Get together with a small group. Choose one item on the *It's Not Fair* list, or decide on an unfair situation of your own. Talk about how you could act out the situation. Assign a role to each person in the group. When you have had time to rehearse, present your "Unfair Situation" to the class.

Inform your classmates that you will be ready to answer questions for five minutes at the end of the presentation. Ask your teacher or a student in your group to lead the question-and-answer session. Questions should be about your presentation. Anyone in the group can offer to answer a question.

TIP When you're answering questions, state your opinion clearly and give a good reason for it!

Class Survey

Find out how many students agree or disagree with the opinions in *It's Not Fair*. Design a questionnaire to survey the class. For each opinion, offer two choices:

☐ Agree   ☐ Disagree

Collect the completed questionnaires. Count the number of answers in each of the two choices. Display the results in a graph like this one:

Follow up with a discussion of the results. Did the students mainly agree or disagree with the author? with each other? Why?

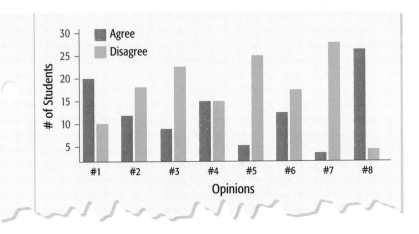

BEFORE READING

In this story, author Jean Little is writing about her own childhood. As you read, make a list of clues that tell you the story took place in the past.

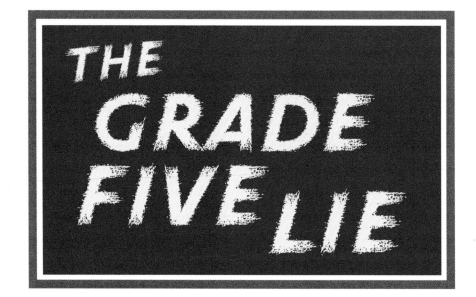

THE GRADE FIVE LIE

I was eating my porridge when Hugh, hurrying too fast, fell down the back stairs. Before Mother could get up, he limped in, sniffling slightly, and displayed a bumped elbow for her inspection. Mother examined it gravely.

STORY BY
Jean Little

PICTURES BY
Terry Shoffner

"A slight hematoma," she said in a serious voice. "And an abrasion almost invisible to the naked eye. You'll live."

Hugh, who always recovered with the speed of light and who won Mother's admiration with his bravery, chuckled at the impressive words.

"What does that mean?" he asked.

"A little bruise and a scrape I can hardly see."

I glowered at my oatmeal. Why did she have to smile at him like that? He was not so special. I searched my mind for something terrible he had done that I could tell her about.

"Jean, hurry up or you'll be late," Grandma said.

I did not want to go to school. We were going to have another mental arithmetic test, and I still did not know my times tables. If only I could fall down and break my leg...

Four-year-old Pat grinned at me.

"Huwwy up, Jean," she parroted. "You'll be late."

I wanted to slap the wide smile off her silly little face. Instead I scooped up a few drops of milk on the tip of my spoon and let it fly. The tiny bit of milk splashed her on the nose. I laughed. Before anyone could stop her, Pat grabbed up her mug filled to the brim with milk and sent its entire contents sloshing over me, soaking me to the skin.

The next thing I knew, I was back upstairs changing out of my wet serge dress, cotton petticoat, long brown stockings, and underwear into clean dry clothes. Not only was this going to make me really late, but Mother handed me the knitted suit Aunt Gretta had made for my tenth birthday. The ribbed blue skirt was sewn onto a sleeveless cotton vest. Over it went a horizontally striped blue-and-pink sweater with short sleeves. Nobody else in Miss Marr's class had a homemade knitted suit anything like it.

"I can't wear it," I said in anguished tones.

"It's lovely," my mother said calmly. "Gretta worked hard to make it for you. Don't be ridiculous. Of course you will wear it."

In ten minutes I was gobbling toast and honey, gulping down milk, and hating my cheerful little sister who was the cause of all the trouble and who got to stay home and be spoiled by everybody.

When I reached the street, it was ominously quiet. I really was going to be late, and it was all Pat's fault. I ran the first three blocks, but slowed down when I got a stitch in my side. There was still not a single child in sight.

As I passed St. John's School, I could hear the grade four class singing "God Save the King." I sent the small building a look of longing. Mr. Johnston had not had these horrid mental arithmetic tests.

Then I stood stock still. When I got to school, Miss Marr would tell me to put my name on the board to stay after four. I didn't mind staying late—lots of the others got detentions—I wasn't sure what to write, though I had a strong suspicion that you did not write out your whole name. Did you just write your initials? Or one initial and your surname? Or your first name and your last initial?

I had to get it right. The others still called me names when no teacher was near enough to hear. The only game I had ever been invited to play was Crack the Whip, and they always made me go on the end. Then, when the big girl at the front swung everybody around in a long Crack!, I ended up flying through the air and landing with a jarring crash on my hands and knees. As I picked myself up, I'd try to look as though I thought crash-landings were fun. Nobody was fooled.

If I wrote my name up there differently than the others did, they would have a new thing to tease me about. I could hear the jeering voices already.

"You're not just cross-eyed, you're so *dumb* you don't even know how to write your name on the board!"

I stood there, thinking hard. How could I save myself? Once in a while, when a child brought a note from home, he got out of putting his name on the board. Well, my mother would not write me a note.

Perhaps, if your parents were not at home, and some emergency cropped up and you had to deal with it, Miss Marr just might let you sit down without asking for a note. It would have to be a desperate emergency...

I began to walk again, taking my time. I had to invent the most convincing lie of my life. Bit by bit, I worked it out. As I imagined how it must have happened, it grew so real that I began to believe it myself. I had every detail ready as I turned the last corner. Then I began to run.

I knew it was essential that I be out of breath when I arrived.

I dashed up the stairs, puffing hard. I opened the door, said a private prayer for help, and entered the grade five classroom. Miss Marr was at her desk. Out of the corner of my eye, I could see monitors collecting the test papers. So far so good.

"Jean," said my teacher, "you're late."

"Yes," I panted, facing her and opening my eyes wide so that I would look innocent and pitiful. "I know. I couldn't help it."

"Why are you late?" she asked.

I took a deep breath.

"Well, I was all ready in plenty of time. But just as I was going out the door, the telephone rang. I knew I should not go back to answer it, but you know my mother and father are both doctors and I was afraid it might be an emergency."

Miss Marr opened her mouth to ask a question, but I rushed on, not giving her time to get a word in edgewise.

"The trouble was, you see, that nobody was home but me. So I took the receiver off the hook and I said, 'Dr. Littles' residence.'"

Everybody was listening now, even the boys who never paid attention. I kept going.

"MY DAUGHTER IS DYING! MY DAUGHTER IS DYING!"

I saw my teacher jump as I shrieked the words at the top of my lungs. Her eyes were wide with shock. The class gasped. I did not stop for effect. I could not give the teacher time to interrupt.

"It was a man's voice. He sounded frantic with worry. 'I'm sorry,' I told him, 'my parents are out. If you call back, they should be home in one hour.' 'No! Please, don't hang up,' he begged. 'You must come and save her life. If I wait for your parents, she will surely die.' 'Well, I guess if she is dying, I'd better come. Where do you live?' I asked him. '111 King Street,' he told me."

Miss Marr did not even try to ask a question as I paused to catch my breath. The entire class was sitting spellbound. The silence was absolute. Not a desk seat squeaked. Not a giggle broke the hush.

"I hurried in and got the right medicine from the office and then I ran out the door. I didn't go the long way around by the Norwich Street bridge. I was afraid it would take too long. I went down London Road and across some stepping stones down there. When I got to King Street, there was the house. It was a log cabin with wind whistling through the cracks. And as I came up to it, I saw the door was standing open and there were a bunch of people in the doorway and they were all crying, 'What's wrong?' I asked them. 'You are too late,' they sobbed. 'She's dead already.'"

This time, as I snatched a breath, Miss Marr choked back a small sound. She made no attempt to stem the flood of my story. I pressed on.

"'Oh, I am so sorry,' I told them. 'Take me to see her.' So they took me into the cabin and there lay the girl on a trundle bed. Her face was blue and her eyes had rolled up till you could just see white and her teeth were clenched. And her fingers and toes all curled over backwards."

I watched Miss Marr carefully at this point, because I was not absolutely sure what a dead person looked like. The last bit worried me especially. I had heard someone say that when people died, they turned their toes up. That could only mean that their toes curled over backwards, but I was not sure about the fingers.

Miss Marr's face quivered a little and her mouth twitched, but she did not speak. I hurried, eager to finish. It would be a relief to sit down. Even so, in spite of myself, I kept putting in extra bits as they occurred to me.

"'She's not quite dead,' I cried. 'She's just on the point of death. I think I can save her.' I hit her chin and her mouth opened. I poured in the medicine. She fluttered her lashes and turned a normal colour and said weakly, 'Where am I?' I turned and hurried toward the door. But before I could escape, all the weeping people went down on their knees and grabbed hold of my skirt and they said, 'You saved her life! We want to give you a reward. Gold, silver, a bag of emeralds, a horse that will come when you whistle...tell us the one thing you want more than anything else in the world and you can have it.'"

I paused for effect this time. I knew no one would break the hush. I wanted my teacher to take in the next bit.

"'The one thing I want more than anything else in the world,' I told them, 'is to be on time for school.' So they let me go and I ran down the hill and across the stepping stones. When I got to the third last stone, though, I slipped and fell in the river and cut my knee. I had to get to shore, go home and bandage my knee and put on dry clothes. Then I hurried here as fast as I could. And that is why I am late."

There was a stunned silence in the classroom. Miss Marr and I stared at each other for a long, long minute. I waited for her to tell me to write my name on the board. Instead she pointed her finger at my desk. Speaking extremely slowly and wearily, she said, "Take...your...seat. Just...take...your...seat."

I tried to keep a solemn expression on my face. But it was hard not to grin. I sat down and did not turn my head as a buzz of whispers broke out behind me. I had missed the mental arithmetic test. I had not had to write my name on the board. And I had kept every single person transfixed with my exciting story.

At least three blissful minutes went by before I realized I had no cut on my knee and no bandage, either. Not only that, but I could not remember whether I had told her which knee I was supposed to have cut.

She had believed me. I was sure of that. Yet any second she was going to discover that I had told her a stupendous lie.

I hooked one knee over the other and clasped my hands around the knee on top. I spent the entire morning that way. When I was required to write, I used only one hand. Miss Marr did not ask me a direct question. When recess time came and she said, "Class, stand," I stayed where I was.

"Jean, aren't you going out for recess?" she asked when the others had marched out and there I still sat.

"Oh, Miss Marr," I said in my smallest, most pathetic voice, "I am so tired from saving that girl's life that I have to stay in and have a rest."

Still clutching my knee with both hands, I laid my head down on my desk and shut my eyes.

She did not say a word.

At noon, when she had her back turned, I ran out of the classroom, dashed home, sneaked bandaids from my parents' office and plastered them over both knees, to be on the safe side. When I returned to school, Miss Marr smiled and did not ask why both my knees were bandaged.

I sat through the afternoon thinking over what had happened. Did she really guess? The other kids did not seem to have figured out that I had lied. One girl had even smiled at me, as though she might be my friend. Nobody in my class had called me cross-eyed. A boy in grade seven had, though. If only I could shut him up the way I had hushed everybody that morning.

Then I remembered Hugh's knee. That night I asked Mother, "What are the long words for what's wrong with my eyes?"

I was standing beside her chair. She looked up at me.

"Why?" she asked.

"I want to know, that's all. They call me cross-eyed. I want to know the long words, the ones doctors use."

She rhymed off a whole list.

"Say it again. Slowly."

"Strabismus, nystagmus, corneal opacities, and eccentric pupils."

I practised.

The next day I was late coming out of school. The same grade seven boy was waiting for me. He had his first snowball ready.

"Cross-eyed, cross-eyed," he chanted and waited for me to start running so that he could chase me, pelting me with hard-packed snowballs.

I turned on him instead.

"I am not cross-eyed," I said in a strong, clear voice. "I have corneal opacities and eccentric pupils."

I glared at him as I spoke, and my eyes were as crossed as ever. But he was so surprised that he stood there, his mouth gaping open like a fish's.

Then I turned my back and walked away. Perhaps his aim was off because he was so used to firing his missiles at a running target. But the first snowball flew past me harmlessly. The second exploded with a smack against a nearby tree.

I kept walking, chin in the air.

In the last two days, I had learned a lot about the power of words. Snowballs would hit me again and I would run away and cry. I would be late and, eventually, I would even have to write my name on the board.

But I had found out what mere words could do. I would not forget.

When do you think this story took place? Compare your list of clues with a partner's list. Then, as a class, decide on a possible date.

Personal Response

• Did you enjoy reading the story Jean made up to avoid getting a detention?

• Do you think her teacher, Miss Marr, really believed this story?

• Should Jean have been punished for telling a lie? Explain your opinion.

School in the Old Days

Find out from parents or grandparents what it was like when they went to school. Have you heard of all the school activities in the list below? (Most of them are in Jean Little's story.) If not, ask the grown-ups to fill you in!

Understanding the Story

The Power of Words

In the story, Jean learns several important ways that words can be powerful. Reread the story to find examples of each of these ways:

• big words can impress or confuse other people

• calling names hurts people's feelings

• a really dramatic lie might be believed

School Activities

mental arithmetic tests

singing "God Save the King"

times tables

detentions

monitors

Crack the Whip

Red Rover

spelling bees

Design a Poster Campaign

Name calling is one of the most unfair things people do to each other. Talk about why this is true. Then design a poster that communicates your concern. You will need both words and pictures to get your point across. Display the posters to end name calling in your class.

Something To Think About

The words you say send messages about yourself. What message do you send about yourself when you

- insult another person? praise another person?

- speak loudly? speak softly?

- listen carefully? interrupt or daydream instead of listening?

- call someone names?

The Right Thing

CALVIN and HOBBES

Cartoon Strip by Bill Watterson

RESPONDING
to THE RIGHT THING

Understanding the Cartoon

On the one hand...

- What dilemma did Calvin face in the cartoon?

- In your opinion, what was the best argument he made for cheating on the test?

- What was the best argument he made for not cheating?

- What decision do you think he would have made, if he had had more time?

- What is the joke in the last line?

Solve a Personal Dilemma

How do you make difficult decisions? One way is to make a list of **pros** (arguments for doing something) and **cons** (arguments against doing something). Think of a decision you have to make. For example:

> "Should I go to Billy's birthday party when I have a bad cold?"

> "Should I tell my mother I lost the sweater Grandad knitted for me?"

Then make two lists, one of **pros** and one of **cons**. Read over your lists. Does it help you to make the decision?

Create a Cartoon Strip

Think of another funny story about Calvin and Hobbes. Imagine Calvin explaining a different dilemma to Hobbes. Plan to make at least four drawings, and use speech balloons for their conversation.

TECH LINK
A computer draw/paint program can be used to create your cartoons.

Did You Know ?

To cheat or not to cheat—it's a question of right and wrong. How do you decide what's the right thing or the wrong thing to do? In other words, how do you make moral decisions? That's what you would study in an ethics class.

How Smudge Came

Story by
Nan Gregory
Pictures by
Ron Lightburn

If there's one thing Cindy knows, this is no place for a puppy.

Up goes the puppy, tucked into her bag.

Home goes Cindy.

If there's one thing Cindy knows, it's don't let anyone see. Cindy sneaks upstairs to her room.

"Is that you, Cindy?"

"Yes, Mrs. Watson."

"You're late. Dinner's getting cold."

"Right there, Mrs. Watson." Puppy goes under Cindy's bed.

At the big table, everyone is eating already. Cindy fills her napkin with stew for the puppy.

"No dessert, Cindy?"

"No thanks." Her chair squeaks as she pushes it back.

Up in her room, puppy eats hungrily.

"Dear little puppy," croons Cindy. If there's one thing Cindy knows, this is her dog.

Knock! Knock! on her door. "Cindy?"

Into the closet goes puppy.

The door opens. They never wait for her to answer.

"Cindy, John is drying the dishes. You can put away."

Cindy concentrates on the plates. *Don't break a plate, Cindy. Think about the plates, not the puppy.*

Back in her room, "Oh, puppy, what did you do?" Cindy cleans up after the puppy.

Puppy sleeps under Cindy's covers. If there's one thing Cindy knows, this is her best friend.

Rrrrrrrrrring! Rrrrrrrrrring!

Get up, Cindy. Get dressed. Go to work. What about puppy? Take him along.

Cindy works in a house called Hospice. Dustpans and buckets and disinfectant. Up and down the halls, in and out of all the rooms. Cleaning, cleaning, cleaning. She likes to make things shine.

Into the pocket of her big yellow apron goes the puppy. Out of the closet come the brooms and the mops and the polishers. Up and down the halls goes Cindy. In and out of the rooms.

Here's Jan, who isn't very old, but he is ugly with disease and he is going to die. Sometimes tears trickle out of his nearly blind eyes.

Clank!

"Is that you, Cindy?"

"Yup." In her apron pocket, the puppy whimpers.

"What's that sound, Cindy?"

"What sound?"

"Didn't you hear it?"

Cindy puts the puppy on Jan's bed.

"Oh my, oh my. A puppy."

"Can you see him?"

"Not really. Just a smudge in the dark." Cindy smiles her slow smile.

"Same when I first saw him. Smudge-in-the-dark."

At lunch, Cindy eats her sandwich on the back lawn. Smudge eats a bit of bread and sniffs around. Then back into the apron for the afternoon.

When Cindy gets home, people are shouting.

"Cindy, what's going on in your room? What did you have in your room last night?"

Cindy's not telling.

Her lips are tight and her eyes are squinty. She breathes through her nose.

"Cindy, stop being silly."

Cindy is leaving now. Someone blocks her way. Someone opens her bag. Hands snatch the puppy.

"Smudge!"

"Cindy, be reasonable."

Now that they have the puppy, everyone is reasonable.

"You can't have a puppy. You can't take care of it. You work all day. What would the puppy do all day while you were at work?"

"Take him with me," Cindy says, but they drown her with their words. She tries to tune out. "SPCA*" she hears. "Good home." She will not weep, but tears squeeze by. She starts to hum. "Go to your room, Cindy."

Next day, Jan props himself up.

"Where's Smudge?"

"'What would the puppy do all day? You can't take care. You can't have a puppy.'" Cindy is furious.

Jan lies back.

After lunch, Cindy is back in Jan's room.

"What's SPCA?"

"A place that looks after animals until someone comes to take them."

"To a good home?"

"That's right."

Cindy snorts.

"Where is it?"

"I'm not sure. East side somewhere."

Cindy brings the phone book. "Find it. Please, Jan."

"Cindy, I can't see. I can't read the phone book."

"Who, then?"

"Carmen, maybe."

Cindy finds Carmen in the TV room. Carmen writes the address on a piece of paper. Cindy folds it carefully. It's far away, but Cindy has a bus pass. If there's one thing Cindy knows, it's how to get around.

When a bus stops, Cindy shows the paper to the driver.

---

* Society for the Prevention of Cruelty to Animals

"Take the Number Nine all the way to Knight Street," the driver tells her. "Good luck."

SPCA keeps Smudge in a cage? The floor is hard and cold. He lies on papers!

"Good home!"

At closing time the clerk tells her, "Come back on Saturday at ten if you want the puppy."

"I'm getting Smudge on Saturday," she tells Jan. "They give him away on Saturday."

Saturday is chore day at the group home.

"Cindy, what's wrong? You usually like to clean." Dusting done, Cindy is gone like a leaf in the wind.

She is panting at the desk. "I've come for my dog."

"Which dog is that?"

"My puppy. Small and black. Smudge."

"Sorry. All the puppies went this morning. Come back next week. We're sure to have more."

Cindy sits in the park for a long time, but the hurt won't stop. Every time she breathes. If there's one thing Cindy doesn't know, it's how to find that puppy. *Crying won't help.*

Cindy makes a whistle with a blade of grass between her thumbs. "Here, Smudge! Here, Smudge!"

There's no place to go but home.

"Cindy. There's a phone message."

What does Cindy care for messages? She lies on her bed and hums.

"Cindy, they want you at Hospice House first thing in the morning. You aren't in trouble, are you?"

At Hospice House, everyone is in the living room.

Jan is up. Jan never gets up. Carmen, too! *Is the TV broken? What's going on? Is there trouble?* If there's one thing Cindy doesn't need, it's another scolding. She starts to tune out.

"Cindy, we have something for you. Cindy, look."

Something soft is in her arms. Something cold nuzzles her chin. Cindy opens her eyes.

"Smudge!"

"We'll keep him here," says Jan. "For you, Cindy. For all of us."

If there's one thing Cindy knows, this is the perfect place for a puppy.

Were you right about the kind of trouble Cindy got into when she took a stray puppy home? What surprised you about the story?

Understanding the Story

A Loving Home

- Where did Cindy find Smudge? How did the puppy get his name?

- Cindy is a person with special needs. What do you think they are?

- What is Cindy's job at Hospice House? How does she feel about her job?

- Why do the staff at her group home say she can't keep the puppy? Where do they take Smudge?

- What happens when Cindy goes to the SPCA to pick up the puppy?

- How did Jan and Carmen and the staff at Hospice House solve Cindy's problem?

Did You Know ?

A hospice is a special place for people who are ill and dying. It looks as much like a real home as possible. The staff there make sure that the patients are comfortable and not in pain. Volunteers come to talk to the patients, and sometimes pets are allowed to visit. Hospices try to create a warm, friendly atmosphere for people near the end of their lives.

Critical Response

Why is Hospice House a perfect place for a puppy? Why do you think the people at Hospice House were so kind to Cindy?

IMAGINE!

You think a certain rule or regulation, such as no pets allowed in your apartment building, is unfair. What would you do to change the rule?

Viewing the Illustrations

In this story, Ron Lightburn's pictures tell you some important things that the words don't say. What are some things that you learned from the illustrations? How would you describe the colours and the texture of the illustrations?

Something To Think About

Rights and Responsibilities

Think about this idea: "With rights come responsibilities." In a small group, discuss this example from the story:

> Cindy has been given the right to keep her puppy.
>
> Should she now take some responsibility for looking after it?

Here are some other examples to talk about:

- As a child in Canada, you have the right to free schooling. Do you have any responsibility in return?

- Canadians believe that everyone has the right to be treated equally in our society. What responsibility do people have in return?

YOUR TURN TO WRITE

A Character Sketch

Which of these words and phrases describe Cindy's character?

kind   lazy   helpful   mean   determined

hardworking   conscientious   polite   gives up easily

For each word or phrase you select, think how Cindy demonstrates this characteristic. Find examples from the story. Then develop your ideas into a paragraph describing Cindy.

Prejudice Is Something We Can Do Without

I walk into a store in town
My pockets bursting with money
My needs are like any other
For goods I want to buy in a hurry
The clerk in the store sees my face, the rugged clothes
My feet in mukluks, the headband on my brow

She has immediate ideas of the poor Indian,
The stereotype in progress
She does not know I sense ill will
So gently I turn around and walk out,
Looking for another store

One where the clerk is all smiles, even if it hurts
I have bought out the store,
My pockets empty
Prejudice is something we can do without
Accept me just as I am,
My money, and my identity

Poem by
Rita Joe

Picture by
Patrick Fitzgerald

RESPONDING

to PREJUDICE IS SOMETHING WE CAN DO WITHOUT

Did You Know ?

Personal Response

- Have you or a friend ever felt that a clerk in a store didn't want to serve you? Why do you think the clerk treated you that way?
- What happened to Rita Joe at the first store? Why did the store clerk see her the way she did?
- At the end of the poem, Rita Joe asks us to accept her just as she is. Do you think everyone has a right to be accepted just as they are? Why, or why not?

In the past, Canada's First Nations people were often treated unfairly. They had to give up their land and move to reserves. Some of their customs were outlawed. Children had to attend residential schools far away from their families, where they were not allowed to speak in their own languages. Today Canadians are trying to correct some of these wrongs. Young aboriginal people are again learning their own languages and traditional skills. But we're still a long way from real fairness.

TV Stereotypes

Suppose you heard someone say, "All kids are noisy and sloppy." That person would be creating a "stereotype" of kids—in other words, an overly simple picture of a group. A stereotype is usually misleading and ignores the fact that kids, or any other group of people, are all individuals. Kids may be similar in many ways, but each kid is also different from every other kid.

Some TV shows have stereotyped characters. Look for examples of stereotyping on TV. Discuss whether or not the stereotypes are harmful.

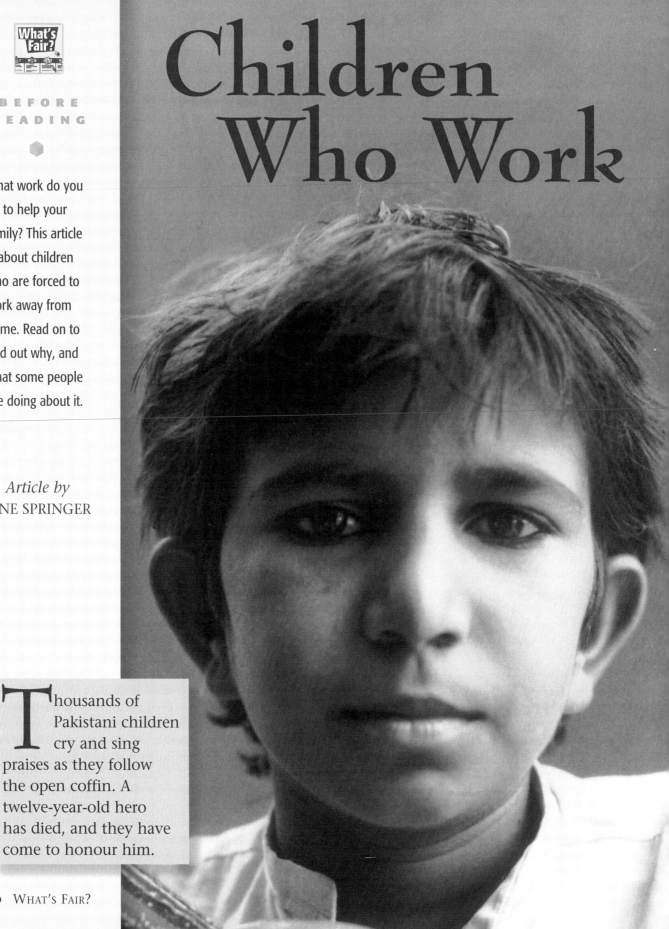

Children Who Work

What work do you do to help your family? This article is about children who are forced to work away from home. Read on to find out why, and what some people are doing about it.

Article by
JANE SPRINGER

Thousands of Pakistani children cry and sing praises as they follow the open coffin. A twelve-year-old hero has died, and they have come to honour him.

Iqbal Masih, born in 1983, lived several lifetimes before he was killed at the age of twelve. His parents sold him for twelve dollars to a carpet-factory owner when he was four years old. As a carpet weaver he was chained to a loom. He worked six days a week, thirteen hours a day. He fought back from the start and was beaten for it.

Iqbal in Boston in 1994.

When he was ten, Iqbal escaped from the factory to attend a Freedom Day celebration held by the Bonded Labour Liberation Front (BLLF), a human rights organization that fights against forced labour. The BLLF told him and other bonded children about their rights. Iqbal was so inspired that he moved to the front of the rally and spoke to the crowd about his experience. He never returned to work as a carpet weaver.

With the help of the BLLF, Iqbal started school and was quickly recognized as a brilliant student. After two years, he became a BLLF activist. In a filmed interview at the time, he stated, "I'm not afraid of the owner any more. Now he's afraid of me."

Iqbal lived in the city of Lahore with his mother, a cleaning woman in a hospital, and his younger sister. He had difficulty breathing and pains in his fingers from his years of work as a weaver. As he told reporters, "The air was full of dust. And if a child hurt his finger, they would dip it in hot oil."

Iqbal worked with the BLLF to help free three thousand Pakistani children from forced labour in carpet, textile, and brick factories, leather tanneries, and steelworks. A compelling speaker, he also brought the plight of working children to the attention of the world. He travelled to Sweden to receive a tribute by the International Labour Organization. In December 1994, Reebok presented him with its Human Rights Youth in Action Award. He planned to use the $15 000 prize money to study law. But he never got the chance.

Craig Kielburger with a photo of an injured boy he met in an Indian firecracker factory.

In 1995, he travelled in India and Pakistan for seven weeks, visiting child workers on the job and even joining a raid to free bonded carpet weavers. He met children making bricks, working in carpet factories, in match and glass factories—hungry, fearful, sometimes tortured, always illiterate.

Members of Free the Children range from eight to eighteen, and chapters have been set up in Canada, the U.S., Australia, Chile, Brazil, India, Switzerland, and Sweden. They have raised $150 000. The money will be used for two projects in India. One is a live-in education centre for freed bonded labourers. The other is a project to set up four schools in rural areas for poor children who might otherwise become bonded labourers. The children will receive a meal a day and a daily supply of grain for their families, which will enable the families to live without their children's income.

Before Free the Children began its work, very few Canadians knew much about child labour. Now, many have some understanding of the issues. Free the Children has also managed another difficult task. It has pressured the Canadian government to take a stand on child labour. Craig's trip to Asia in 1995 coincided with the prime minister's trade mission there. Because Craig was receiving so much publicity, the prime minister was pretty much obliged to meet with him and discuss Free the Children's concerns. Following this meeting, the prime minister agreed the government would take measures against child labour. Free the Children has also convinced the Toronto city council not to buy fireworks produced by children and is working to persuade other cities across Canada to do the same.

"We never even imagined the power we would have to bring about a change," says Craig. "The more people who understand a problem, the sooner a change will come about."

Craig Kielburger, Marilyn Davis, and Brendon Hill from Free the Children.

THE SCHOOL FOR IQBAL MASIH FUND

The School for Iqbal Masih Fund was set up by students at Broad Meadows Middle School in Quincy, Massachusetts. They met Iqbal Masih when he came to their school and told them about his life as a bonded labourer. When they heard only a few months later that he had been murdered, they vowed to help continue his struggle. The kids sent out flyers, wrote letters, and set up a home page on the Internet called "A Bullet Can't Kill a Dream." By the end of July 1996, they had raised $114 000 for the Iqbal Masih Education Centre in Iqbal's home village in Pakistan. It will accommodate two hundred children between the ages of four and twelve—either those who have been bonded child workers or those who risk being sold into bondage. ●

FOLLOW UP

What is so unfair about the way these working children are treated?

A Letter

Is Canada doing enough to help free child labourers around the world? Write a letter to your local Member of Parliament encouraging the member to do everything possible to end the problem. Use the correct letter form. In your letter, be sure to

- state the problem
- give examples of the problem
- state why it is so unfair and unjust
- describe the work of Iqbal Masih and Craig Kielburger
- ask for action to help the cause

Understanding the Article

His Words Touched Our Hearts

- Why do you think Iqbal's parents sold him to a carpet factory?
- What does the BLLF organization do to help working children?
- What did Iqbal do to help his fellow child-workers?
- In what ways is Iqbal a hero?
- What did Amy and Amanda do after Iqbal visited their school?
- How has Craig Kielburger tried to help working children around the world?

Hold a Fund-Raiser

With your class, plan, organize, and run a fund-raising event to raise money for Free the Children. Think about bake sales, book-a-thons, walk-a-thons, and other events. Select an event you would enjoy that will make money. At the same time, be sure your event informs people about the importance of the cause.

"Declaration of the Rights of the Child"

CLASS DISCUSSION

In 1959, the United Nations declared that every child should have

1. equal rights, regardless of race, colour, sex, religion, or nationality
2. a chance to grow up in a healthy and normal manner, in freedom and dignity
3. a name and a nationality
4. good nutrition, housing, recreation, and medical services
5. special treatment, education, and care if physically, mentally, or socially challenged
6. a home filled with love and understanding, with parents whenever possible
7. free education and recreation
8. protection and relief in times of disaster
9. protection against all forms of neglect, cruelty, and exploitation
10. an upbringing in a spirit of understanding, tolerance, friendship among peoples, peace, and universal brotherhood

These are not laws that can be enforced. But the UN wanted to encourage governments around the world to make laws so that each child could enjoy these rights. Most people today agree with the Rights of the Child, but many children still suffer in one way or another.

Discuss:

- Do you agree that children should have all of these rights?
- Which of these rights are violated when families have to sell their children as bonded workers?
- In Canada, who is responsible for protecting the rights of children?
- Do you know of any cases in Canada where children's rights are violated?

The family in this story is faced with the possibility of having to leave their home. Read to find out how they deal with the problem.

The Saltbox Sweater

STORY BY *Janet McNaughton*
PICTURES BY *Janet Wilson*

Katie woke to the growl of heavy equipment. Oh no, they'd started! Pulling on her clothes, she tore outside and up the hill. Mom and Nanny Grace were already there, watching. Uncle Len and his family had their car packed for the mainland. The backhoe pushed. Katie's mother put her arms around her. The old saltbox house groaned, then collapsed. It was over so soon.

"Poor house," Nanny Grace said. "Gone after almost two hundred years."

"Now, Mom," Uncle Len said, "don't cry. It's for the best. I couldn't bear to have the house rot away. I'll call from Toronto." He looked anxious to leave.

Their car disappeared down the winding road. Since the fish plant closed last year, half the families in Quiet Cove had left Newfoundland for the mainland, like Uncle Len's family.

"This place seems empty," Nanny said as they walked down the hill. "Only new thing is that big grocery store in Carbonear."

"And it's taking Mr. Verge's business," Katie's mom said. "Better hurry if I want to keep my job."

"Mr. Verge won't fire you, Celia," Nanny Grace laughed. "You're the best worker he ever had."

"Well, I only got the job because the Porters moved," Katie's mother said.

Katie said nothing. Betty Porter had been her best friend. Now, she was only a pen pal.

Katie's house was filled with boxes and furniture Uncle Len had carried down yesterday. How would all of Nanny's things fit in?

"Help me unpack while your mother works, Katie," Nanny Grace said. Katie nodded. Unpacking would keep Nanny's mind off the saltbox house. Katie opened a box of old photos.

"That's your great-great-grandparents on their wedding day," Nanny said. "Grandfather Edwin made this day bed for Annie, his bride." Nanny pointed to the old couch. "It's been in the saltbox house ever since. Every Johnson baby in Quiet Cove was born in that house until the hospital opened. Now the house is gone." Nanny dried her eyes again.

While they worked, Katie pictured those Johnson babies on the day bed in frilly white clothes. She tried to imagine them smiling, but they wouldn't smile. Not today.

Mom came home upset that night. "Verge's is closing," she said. "Mr. Verge can't compete with that new store. We should have gone with Len."

"No," Katie said. "We belong here."

Nanny smiled. "That we do."

"Well, with my savings and Employment Insurance, we can only stay another year," Mom said.

"Maybe the fish plant will reopen then," Katie said.

"No, Katie. I need to find new work. But maybe leaving's not the answer."

When Mr. Verge closed the store, he gave away everything he couldn't sell. "Anything take your fancy, Katie?" he asked.

"Can I look in the loft?"

He nodded.

The loft smelled like mothballs. It was filled with things nobody bought—funny short skirts and bright men's shirts. Nothing for Katie. As she left, she saw three canvas bags tied to a ceiling beam. She untied one and gasped with pleasure. Inside was wool in every colour of the rainbow. She ran downstairs.

"Mr. Verge, can I have this wool?"

"Yes, child. People stopped buying wool when they got electric dryers. Take it and welcome."

Katie carried the bags home in three trips, singing all the way.

"What's all this?" her mother demanded. She sounded angry.

"Just wool." Tears stung Katie's eyes.

"I'm sorry. Don't cry," Mom said, but the wool was put away and forgotten.

That fall, Nanny and Mom picked blueberries and partridge berries and preserved them. Then they decided to wallpaper the rooms and paint the wood trim. The mess was awful but it kept Mom and Nanny busy.

November was too wet for walking. Everything was papered and painted. One night, Katie's mother said, "Grace, why don't you teach me to knit?"

They pulled Katie's wool from the closet. Nanny Grace smiled. "I'll get knitting needles."

Katie's mother's first scarf was lumpy, but Nanny Grace said, "You learn fast, Celia. Let's try stockings." Soon Katie's mother had learned to change colours and make patterns.

"Those socks don't match, Mom," Katie said.

Her mother smiled mysteriously. "That's OK." Soon, stockings were everywhere. No two were alike. What was she doing?

At the Christmas concert, when her choir sang, Katie saw lots of sad faces. Too many people were missing. But Katie's mother wore a smile and carried a big canvas bag. When everyone started to leave, Katie's mother said, "Wait!" She gave every kid a big, bright stocking to hang up for Santa. No two were alike. Everyone left the concert smiling.

All January it rained and snowed. There were still no jobs. Will we have to move? Katie wondered. She didn't ask.

One day, Ms. McGrath from the Crafts Development Association came to Quiet Cove. People showed her the Christmas stockings. She came to Katie's house after supper.

"You have talent," she told Katie's mother. "Come take craft courses in St. John's."

"I'd like to. But we can't afford it."

"You should learn to make sweaters. I'll send you design books," Ms. McGrath said. "You can submit your work for the Christmas craft fair next November."

"Next November? That's a long time." Katie's mother sighed. "I'll try sweaters, Ms. McGrath, but we'll have to move by the end of the summer if I don't make money."

Katie's mother learned to make her own designs. Her sweaters weren't like anyone else's. Knitted fishing boats rocked across stormy knitted seas. Jam jars seemed to hold real fruit.

"These sweaters are special," Nanny said one evening. Katie thought so, too. They sent photographs of the sweaters to Ms. McGrath. Then they waited.

Winter ended. The puffins returned to Bird Rock. One day, Katie found Nanny Grace staring out the window where the saltbox house had stood.

"Teach me to knit?" Katie asked. She learned to make mittens.

No letter came. One day, Katie's mother said, "My sweaters must be too unusual." She folded the sweaters into the canvas bags and put them away.

I don't want to be the last Johnson to leave Quiet Cove, Katie thought. That night, she dreamed about Mr. Verge's store. But instead of groceries, sweaters filled the shelves.

Next morning Katie knew what to do. After school, she went to Mr. Verge's house.

"Could we borrow your store for the summer?"

Mr. Verge laughed. But when Katie explained, he stopped laughing. "Let's talk to your mother," he said.

"Thanks for the offer, Mr. Verge," Katie's mother said, "but I can't pay any rent."

"Just pay the electric bill, Celia. You could sell other people's crafts, too."

"It might be a start," she said. "But if the sweaters don't sell and don't get into the Christmas craft fair, we'll leave after Labour Day."

They called the store "Quiet Cove Crafts." They sold Mr. Hand's wooden whirligigs and Mrs. Carter's rag dolls, too. Katie worked in the store every afternoon.

"Why don't you play outside?" her mother would say.

"I like it here," said Katie. She dusted the shelves and folded sweaters. A few tourists came and money trickled in. Enough money? Katie couldn't ask. She waited for a letter from Ms. McGrath.

Nanny Grace and Mrs. Carter started a tearoom in the store. More tourists came. Katie's mother was knitting a new design, but she kept it hidden. "This one's a surprise," she said.

One weekend, they sold nine sweaters. "Does this mean we can stay?" Katie asked.

Her mother sighed. "Soon the tourists will be gone. We can't get through the winter without the Christmas craft fair."

Katie scowled at the mailboxes. Where was that letter?

Next weekend was rainy. The tourists stayed away. All this work, Katie thought, just to end up moving to a city full of strangers. She hardly noticed the car stopping.

"Oh, hello," Katie's mother said. Katie looked up. It was Ms. McGrath.

"I was away all summer. No one opened my mail. I rushed here to say we love your sweaters! We want you to enter the 'Best New Product' category at the Christmas craft fair. Do you have any new designs?"

Katie's mother smiled. "This was a secret, but..." She opened her bag. There, on the half-finished sweater, was Nanny's saltbox house.

"This is special," Ms. McGrath said.

"Yes, it is," said Nanny Grace. Katie pretended not to see the tears. They were happy tears.

After supper, Katie and her mother walked out by Bird Rock. "Can we stay?" Katie asked.

"Yes, but there won't be much money, Katie."

"That's OK. We belong here."

That night, as Katie fell asleep, she pictured all the Johnson babies in frilly white clothes. Every one smiling, big toothless smiles. ◈

Why did the family want to stay in Quiet Cove? Have you ever had to move when you didn't want to? How did you feel about it?

TIP › Ask a timer to help keep the speeches short. And always keep your cool. Debaters never get really angry!

Informal Debate

In a debate, two teams pick opposite sides of an argument and try to prove that their side is right. Here's how you can hold a debate in class:

1. Pick a statement to be debated, such as:

"It's not fair that unemployed workers have to leave their homes to look for jobs."

OR

"It's not fair that children should be forced to work instead of going to school."

2. Select two students for Team A and the same for Team B. Team A is **pro** the statement; Team B is **con**. Team A thinks of reasons to agree with the statement, while Team B thinks of reasons to disagree with it. (They should be good reasons, but they don't have to be the debaters' real feelings.)

3. To run the debate, begin with the first speaker for Team A. This person gives two or three good reasons to support the statement. Next, the first speaker for Team B gives two or three reasons against the statement. Continue with Team A's second speaker and Team B's second speaker.

4. The first speakers on each team should sum up their team's arguments, and say why they think the other team is wrong. Then have the audience (your classmates) choose the winning team by a vote. The winners are the team who presents their arguments most convincingly (even if you don't agree with them!).

TECH LINK

If you have a key pal from another part of the world, you may wish to discuss these questions on-line.

Home Designs

IMAGINE!

Design a sweater, T-shirt, or sweatshirt with a symbol that means "home" to you.

- Why are so many families, including Uncle Len's, moving away from Quiet Cove?

- Why did Uncle Len have the old saltbox house torn down? Do you think he had a good reason?

- How did the family earn money after Mr. Verge's store closed?

- Why was Mom's secret sweater design so special to Nanny Grace?

- At the beginning of the story, Katie pictured the Johnson babies in frilly white clothes, not smiling. How did this picture change at the end?

Something To Think About

Is it fair that workers who lose their jobs in one part of Canada must move to other parts of the country to find work? Talk about some examples you have heard of in the news. What are some possible solutions to this problem?

MORE GOOD READING

🍁 The United Nations: Its History and the Canadians Who Shaped It
by Desmond Morton

What does the United Nations mean to you? Collecting money for UNICEF? Learn how the United Nations has worked for over fifty years on behalf of people all over the world. (an information book)

🍁 Listen to Us: The World's Working Children
by Jane Springer

If you found the story about Iqbal Masih moving, you'll want to read more about working children and what you can do to help them. (a non-fiction book)

🍁 If Sarah Will Take Me
by David Bouchard and Robb Dunfield

When artist Robb Dunfield came to David Bouchard's school to tell the students about his experiences as a quadriplegic, David decided to write a poem about him and publish it with Robb's paintings. (a poetic picture book)

🍁 Pit Pony
by Joyce Barkhouse

Life is hard in the coal mines of Cape Breton at the turn of the century. Eleven-year-old Willie Maclean doesn't want to work in the mines. Gem, a gentle Sable Island pit pony, helps him. (a novel)

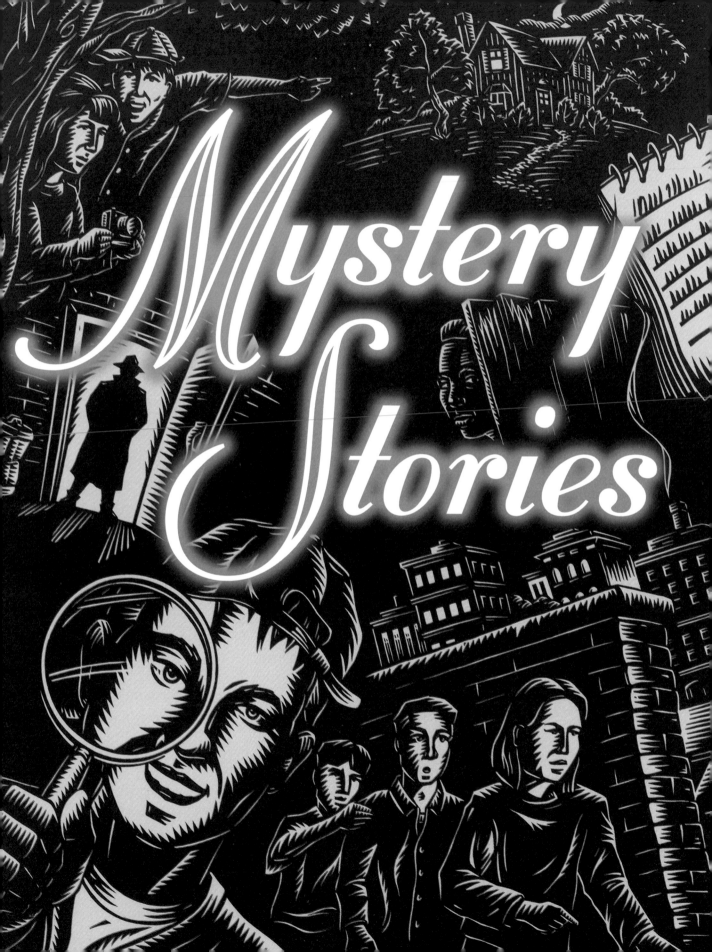

DR. QUICKSOLVE'S *Whodunit Puzzles*

Mini-mysteries by **Jim Sukach**
Pictures by **Lucy Corvino**

BEFORE READING

Here are two mystery puzzles for you to solve. Sorry, we can't give you any clues!

Dr. Quicksolve is a detective who certainly knows his business, solving crimes. Many people are amazed at how he solves so many crimes so quickly. When asked how he does it, he replies, "I'm no smarter than anyone else. I just listen very well."

Read, listen, think carefully, and you can solve these crimes too!

HOLEY DONUTS

Dr. Quicksolve arrived at the scene of the robbery, the office of the Dee Dee Donuts Company. Gerald Cremefil was being questioned by a uniformed police officer, Officer Longshot. Mr. Cremefil was just explaining what happened.

"I was sitting here at my desk. I heard someone come in. Before I could turn around someone hit me on the head. He tied me to my chair and blindfolded me. He had a gun and he forced me to open the safe. He took all the money and then he left."

"Can you describe the robber, Mr. Cremefil?" Dr. Quicksolve asked.

"No, like I said, I was blindfolded," Mr. Cremefil responded.

"What did you do after the robber left?" Quicksolve asked then.

"Well, after he left I rocked my chair back and forth until I fell over. The chair broke, and I was able to untie myself. It probably took me half an hour or so to get loose. When I did, of course, I called the police right away," Mr. Cremefil explained.

"Mr. Cremefil," said Dr. Quicksolve, "I'm afraid there's a hole in your story bigger than the holes in your donuts. Now tell us the truth about this."

Why did Dr. Quicksolve suspect Mr. Cremefil?

SKATING RINK ROBBERY

Dr. Quicksolve entered the skating rink building. You could hear the loud music they played, even in the lobby. In the main room where the skaters skated around and around, you could hardly carry on a conversation because of the loud music.

The manager, Mr. Blade, came over to the detective and signalled for him to come through a nearby door marked "Office." When they went in and closed the door you couldn't hear the music, and they could talk. Two men were sitting in the office. One was holding an ice pack to his head.

"I had this room made soundproof to keep out the loud music the teenagers like so much. The problem is, we've been robbed. I just got here myself, so I'll let my employees, Frank and Joe, tell you what happened. Joe, you go first."

The one with the ice pack spoke up. "I was in here counting the money. I was sitting here with my back to the door and someone came in behind me and hit me over the head. When I came to, the money was gone."

"What can you tell us?" Dr. Quicksolve asked, turning toward Frank.

"I was out in the main room watching the skaters. I heard a crash from the office here, and I turned around just in time to see a tall man slip out of the office and run out of the building. I came in and found Joe unconscious. I woke him and called the police."

"So where did you hide the money so quickly, Frank?" Dr. Quicksolve asked.

Why did Dr. Quicksolve suspect Frank?

Did you solve the mysteries as quickly as Dr. Quicksolve? If so, pat yourself on the back! If not, turn to page 160 to find the answers.

A Mystery Puzzle

Try your hand at writing another mystery puzzle starring Dr. Quicksolve (or a detective you invent). Plan ahead by thinking of these elements of any good mystery story:

- a crime to be solved (theft, smuggling, etc.)
- one or two suspects (people who might have committed the crime)
- a witness to the crime (someone who might have seen something)

- a detective to solve the crime
- a sense of danger, fear, or suspense
- clues as to who committed the crime (fingerprints, dropped clothing, a story full of holes, etc.)
- a solution discovered by the detective

TECH LINK
If you have a key pal, try sending them your mystery puzzle.

Understanding the Selection

Solving Mysteries

- What was the hole in Gerald Cremefil's story in *Holey Donuts*?
- How did Dr. Quicksolve discover that Cremefil was lying?
- What part of Frank's story did Dr. Quicksolve not believe?
- Why do you think the author gave the characters these "punny" names?

BEFORE READING

Preview the article to locate

• the quotes from Linda Bailey's mystery novels

• the titles of her novels

What do you think you will learn from the article?

Article by
SUSAN HUGHES

How Does She Do It?

Linda Bailey reveals her secrets for writing mystery novels!

THE DETECTIVE

I...stared into the mirror again. Staring back was a long thin girl with wild, curly brown hair and a pointy freckled nose. She was wearing black tights (easy to run in and invisible in the dark), a long-sleeved black T-shirt (dead plain and serious, with nothing written or drawn on it), black socks, and black baseball shoes... She looked lean and strong and smart. I knew who she was. I could read it on the label. She was

STEVIE DIAMOND, DETECTIVE.

(from *How Come the Best Clues Are Always in the Garbage?* page 20)

Meet Stevie, pre-teen detective and hero of the Stevie Diamond Mystery series. She sure isn't brilliant. She definitely isn't perfect. But that's the way that Linda Bailey, a Vancouver-based mystery writer, likes it. Stevie is an intelligent girl who is bold, adventurous, and sometimes leaps into things without thinking.

Jessie Kulniki is Stevie's sidekick. He was only a minor character in Linda's first book, but, the writer explains, "He and Stevie started arguing. Suddenly, he was asking if he could be her partner. I was having so much fun writing their argument down that I wasn't surprised when Stevie said 'Yes'!"

The Stevie Diamond books are called "detective stories" or "whodunits." In Linda's opinion, there are a few necessary elements in the detective story: a detective, a crime, some suspects (people who might have committed the crime), and a bunch of clues. Some of the clues lead to the person who did it, while others lead Stevie— and the readers—off track. Although Linda doesn't make a list and check off these elements as she writes, they always seem to "creep in" to her mysteries.

THE CRIME

Every detective story needs a crime. Linda begins each new novel by thinking about a place that might be an interesting setting for a crime. She doesn't put Stevie and Jessie into typically scary settings, such as lonely graveyards or haunted houses. But she does like to take ordinary places and make them scary just by the way she describes them:

> **Take it from me—a greenhouse at night can be a very spooky place. Dead quiet, for one thing, except for strange whooshes from the furnace and sudden flutters among the leaves. Dark, too, with shadows that seem to be waiting, like black holes, for a chance to suck you in.... After awhile, you can't help feeling that things are growing in your direction—hundreds of scrawny tendrils crawling, reaching out like skinny little arms.**

(from *How Can A Frozen Detective Stay Hot on the Trail?* page 78)

Next, Linda starts fantasizing about the kind of crime that might happen in her setting—robbery, smuggling, or...? The best crimes offer a fascinating puzzle for Stevie and her pal Jesse to try and solve:

> **"Maybe somebody forced Gertie to take a holiday," I said.**
> **"People don't force you to take a holiday, Stevie. That would be– "**
> **I nodded.**
> **"Oh, boy," he said.**
> **I nodded again.**
> **"Kidnapping? You're not serious!" he stared at me. Then, "You are serious!...**
> **Why would anybody kidnap a seventy-two-year-old woman with no money?"**

(from *Who's Got Gertie? And How Can We Get Her Back?* pages 33-34)

THE SUSPECTS

In her mysteries, Linda has to make sure that her detective, Stevie, has several suspects to pursue. The stories can get quite complicated with all those characters! Along with Stevie, the readers keep trying to guess which suspect is the right one. Maybe this character committed the crime:

> **Next I spotted a quiet little white-haired woman who was biting her fingernails. Must be feeling guilty about something. After watching her for a moment, I decided it was probably an overdue library book.**

(from *How Can a Frozen Detective Stay Hot on the Trail?* page 34)

Sometimes Stevie is hunting for a really heavy-duty criminal who will stop at nothing to get what he or she wants. She reads about this one in a newspaper article:

> **Ragnall, a master of disguise, is known in police circles as "Rubberface" Ragnall. He is said to have the ability to transform his appearance almost completely… According to police, Ragnall has smuggled millions of dollars worth of illegal items into North America over the past five years.**

(from *How Can I Be a Detective If I Have to Baby-Sit?* page 27)

THE CLUES

Linda drops clues into her stories at just the right spot and just the right time. She explains, "The whole time I'm writing, I know the real story, what really happened at the crime. I let pieces of it slowly slip out, bit by bit. The bits that slip out are the clues. If the reader is working hard and paying attention, he or she may be able to put these bits together and solve the mystery ahead of the detective." Stevie Diamond finds some of the clues pretty yucky:

> **Believe me, if I could have had my *choice* of clues, I would not have picked three plastic chicken heads. I would have chosen a wine glass with a lipstick smear maybe, or a shred of silk clothing, or a smashed watch with the time stopped. Something dignified and elegant. But no—I got chicken heads.**

(from *How Come the Best Clues Are Always in the Garbage?* page 46)

WRAPPING IT UP

Stevie's most satisfying moment comes when she has followed all the clues and solved the crime. Sooner or later, she always finds out "whodunit"!

The Stevie Diamond mysteries are fun to read, but the young detective does get into some frightening situations. Fortunately, readers can take comfort from the fact that Stevie reappears in book after book. The thrill of any mystery series is watching your favourite detective survive and solve the crime, time after time.

Linda Bailey is happy to share many of her insights into the mystery of mystery writing, but she doesn't want to give all her secrets away. As Stevie thinks to herself on the last page of *How Can a Frozen Detective Stay Hot on the Trail?*:

After all, what's the good of being a detective if you can't keep at least one mystery to yourself?

Perhaps the same is true of mystery writers and their tricks of the trade! ⬡

What did you learn from the article? Which of the novels in the Stevie Diamond series intrigued you the most?

Read a Novel

Choose one of Linda Bailey's mystery novels and read it from beginning to end. When you have finished, write up a short report on it—but be sure not to give away the ending! Share your report by pinning it up on a class bulletin board. Here is a form you could use:

Title: _____

Author: _____

Crime to be solved: _____

Stevie's smartest move: _____

Weirdest suspect: _____

Funniest or scariest moment: _____

Best reason to read the book: _____

Understanding the Article

How to Write a Mystery

- How would you describe Stevie Diamond, detective?

- What are the necessary elements in a detective story?

- Why do you think Linda Bailey begins by thinking of a place where the crime could take place?

- What kinds of characters could be suspects in a Linda Bailey novel?

- What are some examples of humour in the quotes from Linda's novels?

- Linda Bailey says she knows what really happened at the crime. How does this help her to drop clues in the right places?

- Why do many readers enjoy reading series of detective novels?

A Detective Story

Now you know the elements of good mystery stories. It's time to write one of your own. Follow Linda Bailey's advice whenever you can. Here are a few suggestions:

- Begin by describing your detective. Give him or her a name, an appearance, a personality, and special interests.
- Next, decide what crime has been committed. Avoid excessive violence!
- Who did it? Decide where, why, and how the person did it. Where is the person hiding now?
- Dream up a few other suspects who could have committed the crime.
- Make a collection of clues that your detective can find.
- Get your detective into a scary situation before he or she solves the case.

You've done your brainstorming. Now just tell a good story!

Did You Know

Suspense is important in mystery novels. It's that feeling of tension that has you asking: "What's going to happen next?" and "How will this character get out of danger?"

"When Stevie gets scared, readers are also likely to feel a little scared," Linda Bailey explains. But it's an enjoyable kind of feeling—and a big part of the reason why mystery stories are so popular.

IMAGINE!

Stevie Diamond becomes the hero of a new TV series. Write to the producers explaining why you and a friend should play the parts of Stevie and Jessie.

BEFORE READING

Readers of detective stories are also detectives. Read this story slowly and look for clues—anything strange or unusual that might be a hint as to "whodunit" and why!

The Red-Headed League

Story by SIR ARTHUR CONAN DOYLE
Adapted by JUDITH CONAWAY

Pictures by LYLE MILLER

WHO'S WHO

Sherlock Holmes: A famous fictional detective, hero of many stories set in England over 100 years ago, written by Sir Arthur Conan Doyle.

Dr. Watson: The narrator who tells the story ("I"). He was a friend of Holmes's, who frequently accompanied the detective on crime-solving expeditions.

Sherlock Holmes still lives in our old rooms at 221B Baker Street. I called upon him there one day last fall.

I found Holmes deep in talk. With him was an old man who had bright red hair.

"Come in, Dr. Watson!" Holmes cried. "Meet Mr. J. B. Wilson. Mr. Wilson, this is Dr. Watson. He works with me on many of my cases."

The old man got up and made me a little bow. Holmes sat back. He put his fingers together. (He often does that when he is thinking.) He smiled.

"Watson, my dear man, I know you love strange stories as much as I do. Mr. Wilson here has just started telling his tale. And it's one of the strangest stories I have ever heard."

Mr. Wilson looked proud. He pulled a piece of paper out of his coat pocket. "Look at this notice, Dr. Watson," he said. "You may read it for yourself."

I took the paper from him.

To All Red-Headed Men

There is a job open at the Red-Headed League.
The pay is 4 pounds a week.
The work is not very hard.
To get the job you must have red hair.
You must be a man over 21 years old.
Come in person on Monday, at 11 o'clock, to 7 Fleet Street.
Ask for Duncan Ross.

"What can it mean?" I asked.

Holmes gave a chuckle. "It *is* a little odd, isn't it? Do tell us more, Mr. Wilson."

"I own a store at Coburg Square," said Wilson. "It's a very small place. Of late years it has not done much more than give me a living. I used to have two helpers. Now I can pay only one. I can pay him only because he will work for half pay. I don't know what I would do without him."

"Hmm. A good helper who works for half pay," said Holmes. "And what is the name of this nice young man?"

"Vincent Spaulding," replied Wilson.
"Oh, Vincent does have his problems. He is always down in the basement. He plays with all those cameras of his down there. A real photo nut. But on the whole he's a very good worker.

"One day about eight weeks ago, Spaulding came into my room. He had this paper in his hand. 'I tell you, Mr. Wilson,' Spaulding said, 'I wish I were a red-headed man. Here's another job open at the Red-Headed League.'

"Now, I had never heard of the Red-Headed League. I don't get out too much. But Spaulding knew all about it.

"He told me that the league had been started by Ezekiah Hopkins. Hopkins was an American millionaire. He had bright red hair.

"All his life people made fun of Hopkins because of his red hair. Then Hopkins came to London. In London he got rich. So he loved London. And he felt sorry for men with red hair. So when he died, Hopkins left his money to the red-headed men of London.

"Now, as you may have noticed, my hair is very red. So it was easy for Spaulding to talk me into giving the job a try. 'What have you got to lose?' he asked me.

"That was a Monday. It's always a slow day at the store. So we shut the shop. Spaulding went with me to Fleet Street.

"I never saw such a sight. Fleet Street was packed with red-headed men. The street looked like a wagon full of oranges. I saw every shade of red you can think of. Orange red. Brick red. Irish Setter red.

"I was ready to give up and go home. But Spaulding would not hear of it. I do not know how he did it. But he pushed and pulled. At last he got me to the door.

"We joined the line going up the steps. There was another line of men coming down. They were men who had been turned down.

"Our line kept moving. Soon we found ourselves in a room on the second floor. There was nothing in the room except two chairs and a table. Behind the table sat a small man. His hair was as red as mine. This man looked over each new job hunter. He found some small reason to say no to each one.

"But my turn was different. The red-headed man took one look at me. Then he got up and closed the door. He shook my hand. 'I'm Duncan Ross,' he said.

"I was too afraid to say anything. So my helper spoke for me. 'This is J. B. Wilson,' said Spaulding. 'He's here about the job with the Red-Headed League.'

"'And he's just right for it!' cried Duncan Ross. 'I don't think I have ever seen such a fine head of hair.'

"Ross stepped over to the open window. 'The job has been taken!' he shouted. One by one the men below all went away. Soon Mr. Duncan Ross and I were the only redheads in sight.

"Ross turned to me. 'How soon can you start your new job?'

"'Uh, I don't know...' said I. 'You see, I have a small store—'

"Vincent Spaulding broke in. 'Oh, don't worry about the store, Mr. Wilson,' he said. 'I can take care of that for you.'

"So I said I would work for Mr. Ross. I was to come to Fleet Street every day between ten and two. My job? Well, you are not going to believe this. All I had to do was copy the Encyclopedia Britannica. That's all. And for that I would be paid four pounds a week!

"I walked out of there feeling very pleased with myself. But not for long. Quite soon I began having second thoughts. This all had to be some kind of joke. I just couldn't believe that story about Ezekiah Hopkins.

"But as my helper had said, I had nothing to lose. So I showed up at Fleet Street the next day at ten.

"To my surprise, everything went just as Mr. Ross had said it would. I went to Fleet Street every day. I copied the encyclopedia. Every Saturday Mr. Ross would come in and pay me four pounds.

"Things went on this way for eight weeks. I copied out all the facts about animals. About apples. About Africa. I began to get tired of the A's. I hoped to finish soon and get on to the B's. Then all at once the whole business came to an end."

"What? To an end?" asked Sherlock Holmes.

"Yes, sir," said Wilson. "It happened only this morning. I went to work at ten o'clock. When I got there I found this card on the door."

The Red-Headed League no longer exists.
October 9, 1890

Sherlock Holmes and I read this card. We looked at J. B. Wilson's face. The funny side of his story made us forget ourselves. We laughed until we roared.

"I can't see that it's very funny," cried Mr. Wilson. His face turned as red as his hair. "If you're going to make fun of me, I'll leave."

"No, no. Don't go," said Holmes. "I very much want to hear your story. I have a feeling it could be something very important."

"Why, of course it's important," said Mr. Wilson. "I have lost four pounds a week!"

"Come, come, Mr. Wilson," said Holmes. "You have lost nothing. You are thirty-two pounds richer than you thought you would be. To say nothing of what you now know about things starting with A."

"But I want to know what it was all about!" Mr. Wilson said. "That's why I came to you, Mr. Holmes. Can you find out for me?"

"I will do my best," said Holmes. "But first—a question. This Vincent Spaulding. This helper of yours. What does he look like?"

"Well, he's small. But very quick and strong. About thirty years old. He has a patch of very white skin on his face."

Holmes sat up straight. He was very excited. "That's enough, Mr. Wilson," he said. "You may go home now. Today is Saturday. By Monday I will have your answer."

When Wilson had gone, Holmes turned to me. "Well, Watson," he asked. "What do you make of it?"

"I make nothing of it," I answered. "It is very strange. What are you going to do?"

"Go hear some music," replied Holmes. "There is a violin concert at St. James's Hall this afternoon. Come along. We have time to make a stop on the way."

We took the underground train to Aldersgate. A short walk, and we were in Coburg Square.

One of the corner houses wore a sign that read "J. B. Wilson." Holmes stopped in front of the house. He thumped on the sidewalk with his stick. He pounded in two or three more spots. Then he walked up and knocked on the door.

Mr. Wilson's helper answered. He was a bright, clean-looking young man.

"So sorry to bother you," said Holmes. "But can you tell me how to get to the Strand?"

"Third right, fourth left," the young man answered. He closed the door.

"That," said Holmes as we walked away, "is the fourth smartest man in London. I have come across him before. Did you get a look at his knees?"

"What about his knees?" I asked. "What do you know, Holmes? Why did you pound the sidewalk like that?"

"My dear doctor," said Holmes. "This is no time to talk. This is the time to look. Let's see what lies behind this quiet block." We turned the corner.

To my surprise, we found ourselves on a busy street. "Let's see," said Holmes. "There's a cigar store. And there's the City Bank. And there is a restaurant...Hmm, yes..."

He turned to me. "I'll want your help," he said. "Can you be ready at ten tonight? Good. See you then. Oh, and Dr. Watson. Do you have your gun? You had better bring it along."

He waved his hand. Then he disappeared.

I got back to Baker Street just before ten o'clock that evening. Two horse-drawn cabs were waiting outside. Inside, I found two men with Holmes.

"Ah! We are all here now!" Holmes said. "You know Inspector Jones of Scotland Yard, don't you, Watson? And this is Mr. Merryweather."

Mr. Merryweather was long, thin, and sad-faced. He wore a very shiny top hat. He did not look at all happy. "This had better not be a wild-goose chase," he said. "I'm missing my Saturday night card game. First time in twenty years."

Holmes laughed. "You'll play a more exciting game tonight," he said. "You, Mr. Merryweather, stand to win or lose thirty thousand pounds. And you, Mr. Jones? You stand to get your man."

"That's right!" cried Inspector Jones. "John Clay. Killer. Robber. He's a young man. But he's at the top of the crime heap.

"Yes—he's quite a man, John Clay. The grandson of a duke. Went to the high-class schools. His head is as quick as his fingers. I've been on his trail for years. I've never even set eyes on him yet."

"I hope you will meet him tonight," said Holmes. "Let's go. Two cabs are waiting outside. You two men take the first cab. Dr. Watson and I will follow in the second."

Holmes did not say much during the long drive. We drove through the dark streets. Soon we got to the busy street near Mr. Wilson's house.

Merryweather and Jones were there ahead of us. We followed Mr. Merryweather down a narrow alley. There was a side door there. He opened it. Inside was a small hall. At the end of the hall there was a heavy gate. Merryweather opened that too. Then we went down some narrow stone stairs. There was another heavy gate at the bottom.

Merryweather stopped to light a lamp. He opened the gate and we passed into a large room. It was piled with boxes.

Holmes held the lamp up to the roof. "Looks as if no one can get in from above," he said.

"Or from below," added Merryweather. He tapped the floor with his cane. "Why—dear me! It sounds hollow!" he cried.

"Quiet now!" whispered Holmes. "Please sit down on one of these boxes. And do try not to get in the way. Your shouting has already put us in danger."

Merryweather looked hurt. But he sat down.

"We have at least an hour to wait," Holmes said. "They will do nothing until our red-haired friend is in bed. After that they will not lose a minute.

"By now, Dr. Watson, I'm sure you know where we are," Holmes went on. "We are in a room under the City Bank. Mr. Merryweather here is the head of the bank. I'll let him tell you why John Clay will soon enter this basement."

"It is our French gold," the banker whispered. "Over thirty thousand pounds' worth." He bit his nails and looked sad. "We were afraid something like this would happen."

"Don't worry," said Holmes. "It will all be over soon. And now we must cover the lamp. I'm afraid we will have to wait in the dark. But first let's get in place. These are very dangerous men. We will have to be careful. I will hide behind this box. You men hide over there. Wait till I flash the light. Then close in on them. Watson, keep your gun ready. If they fire, shoot them down in their tracks."

I bent down behind a wooden box. I kept my gun hand on top of the box. I was ready for anything.

How long that wait seemed! Later I learned that we had waited only an hour and a quarter. But it felt like all night. I tried not to move. I was afraid to make a sound. I could hear the other men breathing.

Suddenly my eyes caught a flash of light on the floor. The flash got larger. It became a yellow line. Then a hole opened. A hand came out of the hole. It was a thin, white hand.

The hand felt the floor around the hole. Then everything went dark again.

But not for long. There was a tearing sound. The hole in the floor got bigger. Over the edge peeped the face of a young man. There was a patch of bright white skin on his forehead. The young man pulled himself up into the room.

A second later he pulled a second young man up. The second man was also small and thin. He had a pale face. His hair was bright, bright red.

At that second Sherlock Holmes flashed the light.

"Great Scott!" yelled the first man. "Jump, Archie!"

"It's no use, John Clay," said Holmes. "You have no chance at all."

Inspector Jones had the handcuffs ready.

"Don't you touch me with your dirty hands," said John Clay. "I have noble blood, you know." The cuffs closed around his wrists.

"You see it all now, Watson," said Holmes. It was early the next morning. We were back at Baker Street drinking tea. "There was only one reason for the Red-Headed League. That was to get our old friend Mr. Wilson out of his store. You may think it was an odd way to do it. But I can hardly think of a better one.

"Of course what gave them the idea was Mr. Wilson's red hair. By chance it happened to be the same colour as Archie's hair. So Archie became..."

"Mr. Duncan Ross!" I cried.

"Quite so. And John Clay became Vincent Spaulding. Remember how he was always in the basement? He said it was for photography. But I knew better as soon as I saw his knees. They were dirty. It was proof that he had been digging.

"Then I tapped the sidewalk in front of the house. No—he wasn't digging out that way. So he must be digging toward the back of the house. We walked around the block. And there I saw the City Bank."

Suddenly Holmes laughed. "Do you know what a red herring is, Dr. Watson? It's a false clue that is meant to lead us away from the real clues. Well, you've got to hand it to John Clay. He's not only smart. He's funny. Don't you get it? The Red-Headed League was just a red hairing, all along!"

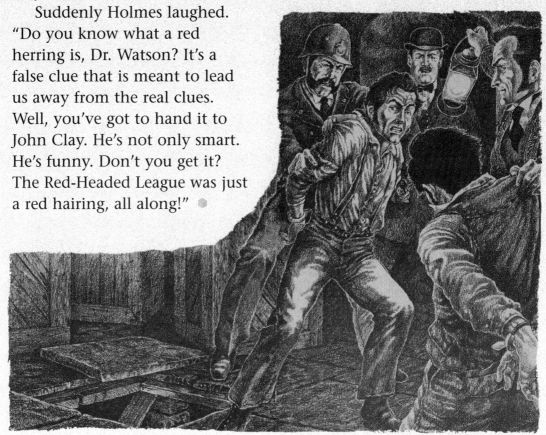

You probably didn't solve the crime before Sherlock Holmes did (few people ever do!). But you probably had a sense that something was fishy. That's half the fun of reading mystery fiction.

Basil Rathbone (right) as Sherlock Holmes.

Jeremy Brett as Sherlock Holmes.

Understanding the Story

The Clues to the Case

- What does Mr. Wilson tell Sherlock Holmes about the Red-Headed League? Why did he come to Holmes for help?
- What clue first made Sherlock Holmes suspicious of Vincent Spaulding?
- What does Holmes learn when he pays a visit to Wilson's home?
  - Who is Inspector Jones, and why has he been called into the case?
  - Who is Mr. Merryweather, and why is he displeased?
  - In this story, the detective managed to stop the crime from taking place. What was the crime, and how did Holmes prevent it?
    - What two characters had false identities?
    - How did Holmes use these clues to solve the case?
      - Spaulding's dirty knees
      - the patch of white skin on Spaulding's face
      - tapping the sidewalk in front of Wilson's house
      - Mr. Wilson's red hair
  - Explain the pun in the last paragraph.

Readers' Theatre

This story is fun to present as readers' theatre. Organize groups of seven students. Decide who will read each part: Sherlock Holmes, J. B. Wilson, John Clay (Vincent Spaulding), Archie (Duncan Ross), Inspector Jones, and Mr. Merryweather. The seventh person is Dr. Watson; this person reads Watson's lines and also takes the part of the narrator. Practise your parts separately and then as a group. If you can, find appropriate hats for each character. When you are ready, perform the story for the class.

 Have each character introduce himself at the beginning. Then leave out phrases such as "he said" and "Holmes cried," since the audience will know who is speaking.

 # TV Reporting

You are a TV reporter. You have been sent to interview one important character from this story. Make up at least six questions that will help you find out what he knows about the case. Then for each question, write the character's answer based on what happens in the story. With a partner, rehearse the interview, then tape it (either on audio or video).

 A reporter's questions always cover **Who? What? When? Where? Why?** and **How?**

BEFORE READING

In the introduction to these mysterious drawings, you will read about the equally mysterious artist, Harris Burdick.

The Mysteries of Harris Burdick

INTRODUCTION

I first saw the drawings in this book a year ago, in the home of a man named Peter Wenders. Though Mr. Wenders is retired now, he once worked for a children's book publisher, choosing the stories and pictures that would be turned into books.

Thirty years ago a man called at Peter Wenders' office, introducing himself as Harris Burdick. Mr. Burdick explained that he had written fourteen stories and had drawn many pictures for each one. He'd brought with him just one drawing from each story, to see if Wenders liked his work.

Peter Wenders was fascinated by the drawings. He told Burdick he would like to read the stories that went with them as soon as possible. The artist agreed to bring the stories the next morning. He left the fourteen drawings with Wenders. But he did not return the next day. Or the day after that. Harris Burdick was never heard from again. Over the years, Wenders tried to find out who Burdick was and what had happened to him, but he discovered nothing. To this day Harris Burdick remains a complete mystery.

His disappearance is not the only mystery left behind. What were the stories that went with these drawings? There are some clues. Burdick had written a title and caption for each picture. When I told Peter Wenders how difficult it was to look at the drawings and their captions without imagining a story, he smiled and left the room. He returned with a dust-covered cardboard box. Inside were dozens of stories, all inspired by the Burdick drawings. They'd been written years ago by Wenders' children and their friends.

I spent the rest of my visit reading these stories. They were remarkable, some bizarre, some funny, some downright scary. In the hope that other children will be inspired by them, three of the Burdick drawings are reproduced here for the first time.

Chris Van Allsburg
Providence, Rhode Island

Under the Rug
Two weeks passed and it happened again.

Mr. Linden's Library
He had warned her about the book. Now it was too late.

The House on Maple Street
It was a perfect lift-off.

FOLLOW UP

Who do you think Harris Burdick was? Why did he bring his drawings to the children's book publisher, Peter Wenders?

Personal Response

- What words could you use to describe these drawings?
- Would the drawings have as much impact if you didn't have the title and caption for each one?
- Do the drawings inspire story ideas in your imagination?

- Which of the drawings is your favourite?

Story Elements – Setting, Character, Event

Each drawing (with its title and caption) gives you a setting, a character, and some kind of event.

SETTING: where and when the story takes place

CHARACTER: a fictional person in a story

EVENT: something that happens in a story

Work with a partner. For each drawing, describe the setting, the character, and the event. Then discuss—what elements would you need to add to make a complete story?

YOUR TURN TO WRITE

A Mystery Story

Choose one of Harris Burdick's drawings (plus title and caption) and turn it into a story. Work alone or with your partner. Here are some ways to get started:

- Give the character a name.
- Explain why the character is in this setting.
- Describe what is happening at the moment.
- Imagine what other character(s) might be involved.
- Tell what happened before this moment.
- Tell what will happen after this moment.

You have ideas for beginning the story, telling about the problem the character gets into, describing the very strange event in the picture, and writing an ending. Now let your imagination go. Write a bizarre, funny, or downright scary story, just as Harris Burdick might have hoped you would!

MORE GOOD READING

❧ The Mystery of the Gold Ring by James Heneghan

James Heneghan has experience in crime—he's a former police officer and fingerprint expert. In this novel, his three detectives, Clarice, Sadie, and Brick, are on holiday in Greece when a mystery falls into their laps. The gold ring of the Minotaur has been stolen! (An O'Brien Detective Agency Mystery novel)

Stories to Solve and More Stories to Solve by George Shannon

These books contain some fascinating mini-mysteries. They're based on folk tales from around the world. The puzzles are challenging to solve, but they are also fun to read and have terrific illustrations. (Short-story puzzles)

Mysteries of Sherlock Holmes by Sir Arthur Conan Doyle Adapted by Judith Conaway

If you liked *The Red-Headed League,* this collection of stories is for you. It includes two other Sherlock Holmes stories, including such famous titles as *The Adventure of the Speckled Band* and *The Adventure of the Blue Carbuncle.* (short stories)

❧ How Can a Frozen Detective Stay Hot On the Trail? by Linda Bailey

Stevie and Jessie are hot on the trail again. This time they are in Winnipeg to clear Jessie's teenage uncle, who has been accused of stealing valuable carnivorous plants. Can they crack this case before winter puts them in the deep freeze? (A Stevie Diamond Mystery novel)

ANSWERS:

Holey Donuts (page 133)
Mr. Cremefil claims he opened the safe after he was tied up and blindfolded.

Skating Rink Robbery (page 134) Frank said he heard a noise from the soundproof office while he was in the main room with the loud music.